STRESS NO EVIL

TWELVE TIPS TO KEEP FROM GOING BANANAS

Bobbe White
Speaker, Author, CLL-E*, NOCW**

Illustrated by Laura Gramke

Cover design by Bill Beard

*Certified Laughter Leader Expert
**No Other Credentials Whatsoever

Printed in the USA by
The White House Press
Quincy, IL

dedication

To Jeff, my husband for forty-four years. He is my on-site advisor for endless predicaments. I call him "Google on Legs." (He knows a lot.) This book is also dedicated to my off-site advisors: Korey, Spencer, Nick, and Jenna. Collectively and individually, they are the best kids ever! You all have tolerated, coached, and survived my most frazzled moments. And still love me. Thanks for being mature enough to parent the parent. Love you all "two pizzas!"

PAWDICATION
Lily White was our black Lab and therapeutic tool for almost fourteen years. Then the kids left, her duck hunting career ended, and she hung out with me. We hope there are endless slices of American cheese and TV remotes to eat in doggy heaven. Then a little Snow fell into our lives in December 2020. She's my new office assistant and therapeutic pup-tool-in-training. She already has reduced my stress, except when she steals stuff, like my toothbrush, from the bathroom.

IN MEMORY
For my parents, Shirlee and Irv Schecter ("ShIrv.") We tend to manage stress much like our parents did, which is inherited and learned. (It'd be great to unlearn the ways that don't serve us well...) On the plus side, Dad's stress tool was golf; Mom's was a six minute power nap. Both are excellent tools. Finally, I'll always be grateful for Mom's ability to stand like steel during crises.

ONE BANANA, TWO BANANA, THREE BANANA, FOUR
Writing is not a one-banana effort, at least not in my neck of the jungle. Thankfully, I found expertise in the following super-proofers and contributors: Nick, Jenna, Korey, Spencer, Diane Earhart, Tracy Schlepphorst, Monica Hinkamper, Mary Beth McGee, Andrea Copenhaver, Karyn Buxman, Lisa Pemberton, Christine Cashen, Connie Hornsey, Pattie Paxton, and Kevin Hannant. If you were overlooked, I'm so

sorry. A lot of life happened between the book's start and the finish. I'll keep better notes next time. That's my only excuse. Thanks to licensed professionals for your guidance and contributions. They are: Penni Ippensen, LCSW, Anne Vahle, MAED, LCPC, and Shirley Longlett, LCSW-retired. Your expertise gives my book more credibility. Friends can't treat friends, but if they could…

Anne Vahle, MSEd, LCPC
Mindshift Center, LLC
web: www.mindshisftcenter.org; email: annevahhlelcpc@gmail.com

Penni Ippensen, LCSW Therapist
ph. 217-228-6193
web: www.pitherapy.org; email: pitherapy@sbcglobal.net

Shirley Longlett, LCPC-Retired

A heartfelt thanks to everyone who helped me!

Writing on stress carries a responsibility. I do not feign professional expertise. I only offer simple ideas for managing life's daily irritations. Stress hops in the car, for instance, when you're running late to your child's ball game. On the way, your child remembers it was your turn to bring treats. Grrrrr. Or how about the stress you felt that morning when pulling into the office parking lot? You noticed there were more cars than usual. Oh no! Oh yes. That meeting started thirteen minutes ago. We may regroup and move on, but not without some stress in the process.

When life's battles befall you, my hope is that you might consider one of the ideas from this book and be further inspired to brainstorm additional ideas to explore.

Application of simple ideas is all many people need to maintain relative calm. Others may experience more serious issues that can cause problematic behaviors. If your stress—or that of someone close to you—is out-of-control and potentially dangerous, please seek the help of a licensed professional or call your local emergency services.

chapters

Read this book in order...or not. You choose!

Q: Do we really need another book on stress?
A: I think so. We need to have many stress management resources, because we're all different.

Q. Who should read this book?
A. Everyone! The material is applicable to many demographics and interests. Those with busy brains and schedules are apt to experience stressful situations—which includes all of us.

Q: Who has time to read this stuff?
A. Nobody. Think of this book as a bathroom primer (e.g. pick it up, put it down, and pick it up again.) Grab it when you're in the tub or on the throne. Do you complain about not having enough time? I just found some for you. You're welcome!

Q: Were others consulted or are these all your ideas?
A: Three mental health professionals reviewed, corrected, and contributed to the content. They're quoted throughout the book. Sources are cited on outside information, as needed.

Q: Explain the poll?
A: I posted a one-question poll on social media:"In six words or fewer, how do you manage your stress?" Missed the poll? List your six on the poll page. Check out the many ways others cope—which, of course, is the general idea of this book!

Q: What causes me stress?
A: I asked our daughter, Korey, "What's the source of my stress?" She said, "Busy Bobbe, you do too many things at once. You run late, never finish anything, and try to help everyone all at one time without prioritizing." Holy Baldy, she nailed it!

Q: Does the content consist of all tips?
A: No! There are quotations, professional opinions, facts, and real-life examples throughout the book. The first story is found on the next page. Enjoy!

"All Stretched Out"

Madelyn and Brooklyn's grandparents, Maw and Paw, thought it was a perfect evening to go get ice cream. Apparently, everyone else thought so too. The Dairy Dipper was packed. Adults fussed and cussed at the long lines. Kids squirmed and fidgeted. Eventually, everyone got their treats.

When the girls returned home afterwards, Madelyn and Brooklyn's mom, Kasey, asked: "How was the ice cream?"

Madelyn said, "Maw said Paw can never go again!"

"Oh no! Why not?" Kasey asked.

"Because Maw said Paw gets too stretched out. He stretches me out too."

Basically, stretched out sounded exactly like stressed out to her. It really is a good miss when you think about it. Stressful moments—or entire seasons in life— can stretch our patience, mindset, and health. Feeling stretched out reminds me of adults who find themselves sandwiched between their parents and children. You might hear someone say, "I feel like my arms are getting longer, because I'm being stretched in so many directions!" Don't you love the accidental wisdom of a five-year-old?

Stress No Evil, the monkey on the cover doing yoga, (i.e. legs folded, hands in prayer position) helps to calm and reposition our minds and bodies. Yoga isn't the answer to everything stressful, but if not well managed, our physical and mental health can be compromised. Stress No Evil reminds us to deal with the negativity of stress.

The Three Wise Monkeys are also on the cover. For more information, see the section later in the book called, "History: Three Wise Monkeys"

And the bananas? Monkeys love bananas. We used them to illustrate our stress tools.

Did you say, "Sex tools?" For some reason, whenever I say, "stress tools" in my presentations, some attendees look at me wide-eyed. Others giggle. They think they heard "sex tools." Hey, use these however they serve you best! I don't care.

YOU'RE **stressed out?** *I'M* **stressed out. We're** *ALL* **stressed out!** These phrases are so worn out. We've become unphased by them. When stressed out or so busy, are we complaining or are we secretly proud of this status? Is it a badge of honor? Busy-ness can be mistaken for productivity. If we're not busy, are we slackers? If we're not stressed enough, are we not all in? I'm not sure. We're just all different. I've said, "I'm *sooooo* busy!" And so have you. Was it a cry for help, such as, "Can you help me out over here?" Was it for reassurance to find out if I was doing a good job? Then again, maybe I was *sooooo* busy! Remember that busy-ness and productivity can happen in the absence of the other.

"Instructing players to handle stress and anxiety is a daily challenge, so I teach "cross-over to life skills." We all have many demands and wear many hats. We are expected to display courage, patience, knowledge, and empathy while wearing each of them. People expect us to deliver these qualities as players, coaches, business people, or family members. We need to make sure that our behavior and actions match our goals."

—Monica Hinkamper, USPTA/USPTR
Tennis Professional & Coach; GM & Director

Like road signs, the monkey icon will point out hot tips, quotes, and ideas we don't want you to miss.

The banana icon will also indicate points of interest.

Thanks for hanging around with me throughout the introductory pages.

Let's stop monkeying around and swing into our twelve tips, shall we?

Stress no evil

This first letter represents two tips with opposing ideas and possibilities. It's a two-for-one tip!

SILENCE AND **S**OUND

<u>S</u>ILENCE

Minimizing noise changes your environment and can have a quick and calming impact on your system.
—Bobbe White, CLL-E, NOCW

Michael Jackson sang, "*Beat It!*" When life gets too noisy, switch "mute" for "beat" and just mute it! Click off the clatter. When home is noisy, you can't turn the kids or the dog off, but you can buy kid-canceling headphones. In public, you can't mute loud humans or traffic noises. So, in order to ease stress from noise, you must get creative to minimize it.

Finding quiet

- **Occasionally, when you are in your vehicle,** cut the Spotify, podcasts, or radio and drive in complete silence. Being enveloped by the quiet is calming. If you've forgotten what calm feels like, this may give you a good idea of it! You'll also be able to hear the engine purr. It's not purring? It's growling? Great! If it hadn't been quiet, you may have missed the noise, resulting in possible repairs and inconveniences.

- **Cop a squat** on the porch, deck, or steps. Enjoy the quiet in any weather. I rarely know what creature is singing, chirping, or burping, but I enjoy their sounds. Right now, doves are singing. That's what Jeff said they were. I wouldn't know a dove song from a dishpan, but the sound is delightful.

- **Water**
  - **Swimming suits me!** I find solace in the swish-swash sound when swimming underwater. Those who don't like having their ears beneath the surface might consider other ways to enjoy water. After rough school days—from grade school through college—I resolved, or at least reduced, stress by the end of swim practice. And yes, there *is* grade school stress. Combining the benefits of quiet with physical exertion results in a powerful two-punch attack on stress.

  - **Bathing** can be quietly calming (especially when you can shut the door!) Fortunately, baths can also be— and probably should be—daily!

  - **Sensory deprivation tanks.** You can float in a small tank of magnesium and sulfate-rich Epsom salts at float spas. It's like floating in the ocean for 30-90 minutes. The air and water temperatures match and you wonder, "Am I floating on water or in air? I can't tell!" Other sensory signals (i.e. light and sound) are minimized, giving you time and space to think, meditate, or sleep. Claustrophobic? Some spas have open pools.

- **Multi-purpose spaces** (e.g. libraries, museums, botanical gardens, parks, and lookout points) are generally quiet and visually pleasing places. Read, listen to music, write, chat quietly, study, or even sleep.

- **Chapels** may be open to the public, particularly in hospitals, as well as memory gardens. There aren't rules on what you must think about. Sort it all out or choose to just be still.

<u>S</u>OUND

Awake or asleep, Jeff likes noise. If I try to sneak the T.V. remote away from him when he's napping, he instantly tightens his grip and says, "Hey, I was watching that!" Interpreted, this means he likes napping to noise. Jeff's iPhone and iPad are always sounding off, "BING! DING! RING!" The dog barks. I bark. I'm convinced that he finds noise relaxing.

Is noise soothing? It can be. What is soothing is individualized. Music, coffee shops, city noise, or people chatting* can all be soothing. We can get lost in noise, but in a good way. Imagine while driving, a good song comes on your device or radio. You crank up the volume and sing every word (actual or improvised!) Drum it out on the steering wheel. It's a personal concert! You feel *GOOOOD!* You sound *GOOOOD!* (You really don't, but it doesn't matter.)

Is your home office soul-crushingly quiet and lonely? Use apps that simulate chatting, typing, water/coffee pouring, phones ringing, and even that little toot noise chairs can make when you shift positions. And there's that follow-up sound as you shift again, proving it the chair tooted, rather than you!

Music rocks! Explore genres to determine what music resonates with you. Choose from acoustic chill to heavy metal; whatever calms you. Sing in the shower! Dance with the dog! Hum in the Honda! Music, song, and dance activate your feel good hormones, called endorphins. Don't worry about feeling silly when singing and driving—unless a car pulls up next to you at a stoplight. Who cares? Just smile, wave, or wink. They'll often reciprocate and feel better too. Your entire body benefits when it's moved by music.

"We hit some West Hollywood clubs—before COVID. I'm a terrible dancer, but it was total freedom!"
—Kevin Hannant, Playwright, dad with two left feet

Calming noise—also referred to as white noise—is available in many on-line apps and programs. It can mask those sudden noises that can frustrate light sleepers. Online apps and devices are abundant.

- **Chime in** with the wind. Wind chimes can sound like pleasant tinkling or resonant gongs. Chimes can be made of any number of materials, from bamboo, to pipes, to shells, or bells. Note: be kind if your neighbors mind! Not everybody delights in the same tinkle or gong. If you live too close to neighbors, consider chimes on an app with ear buds.

- **Waterfalls** can be enjoyed indoors! Some are small enough to sit on your bedside stand, or large enough to cover a wall or a patio.

- **Fans or sleep machines** are my family's drug of choice. Personally, I prefer a snoring dog, ticking clock, or crickets outside. We recently traveled and forgot the sleep machine. Jeff downloaded a thunderstorm app and slept like a lamb. I slept like a…basically, I slept very little.

"Our systems remember a time when all was safe and calm. Calming noise can predict a steady input of auditory sounds that block out the unpredictable noises and gives us a sense of safety in predictability."
—Anne Vahle, LCPC, MSEd

s**T**ress no evil

TOXIC AVOIDANCE

You have two basic choices:
- *Stay around toxic people and be miserable*
- *or move right along*

What's toxic to you is not toxic to everyone. How can you tell if you're in a toxic situation or with toxic people? Check-in with your body. You can feel it by doing a gut or pulse check. Something may feel slightly off normal or even miserable—not to mention unhealthy—when we endure toxic humans or places.

- **Learn and avoid your hot spots.** My first grade hot spot involved Lacie (fake name). She mastered intimidation early. You did *not* want to get on Lacie's bad side, but somehow I did. One day I walked by her desk and she said, "I hate you!" I tattled, because that's what you do in first grade. Mrs. Smith made us patch things up, seeing as I walked by Lacie's desk daily. I was at a loss as to how I had offended her. I decided both she and her desks were hot spots for me.

- **Be like a Bose** (stereo system.) Limit toxicity in your world by surrounding yourself with positive people and places. Fill up! Don't drain down! Take a quick inventory. Look around (figuratively or literally) occasionally to consider with whom you're surrounding yourself, as the next quote suggests.

"You will move in the direction of the people that you associate with. So it's important to associate with people who are better than yourself."
—Warren Buffett, CEO Berkshire Hathaway

Why do we stay in toxic situations?

- **No choice in the matter** (You *always* have choices. Is risking your wellness worth it?)

- **I'll hurt/anger others** by avoiding them. While supporting this person seems fine, you're actually enabling someone to behave badly. Working overly hard to protect a relationship can be exhausting. Bad situations don't make good sense!

- **FOMO** (Fear of Missing Out) Typically, the fear is worse than what you'll actually miss.

- **I like some of the people in the group.** Except one bad apple spoils the whole bunch. There's another option when it comes to more than two people. Consider organizing a small group of like-minded people. Gather all of your good apples together and avoid the rotten ones.

- **I'm obligated to help with** _____. Caregiving is one example where emotions can run high. Relatives can get crosswise with each other about the care. This can result in toxicity that spreads faster than a bad case of poison ivy. It may be helpful to have an outsider or professional to intervene and attempt to keep the situation calm.

- **Overall fear.** We know the situation doesn't suit our needs, but we may be too uncomfortable or scared to move on.

"Women may stay in toxic relationships due to fear and abuse. If you are afraid to leave a toxic situation, call 800.799.SAFE (7233), 9-1-1, or contact your mental health professional."
—Penni Ippensen, LCSW-Therapist

When possible, identify toxic situations before entering them. We've all been seated by that *one* person at a wedding or meeting: Blood Boiler, Bubble Burster, or Big Bragger. Will our positive aura bring them up? No, but they can bring us down! They have no idea they're toxic. Strategize before entering! As Deborah Norville, former Today Show host said, "The good news is nothing icky lasts forever."

Dozens of people weave and wind through our careers. Occasionally, I've encountered a difficult person. (I'm never the difficult one, of course. It's always them, right?) Our brushes with the difficult ones are stamped upon our minds forever, like the following story.

"Moxie Roxie"

I once had a supervisor named Roxie. (Not her real name.) She was hired to propel our projects into the twenty-first century and manage areas at which I was less adept. This left me responsible for more preferable duties. That girl, Roxie, had a lot of moxie! She came in like a wrecking ball and micromanaged my efforts. I felt like a second-grade slacker. I should've stood up for myself, but I fell silent. Sadly, this is because I am conflict averse.

My confidence sank. My morale slumped. Coworkers observed my droopy mood. Just in case it was bad *feng shui*, I rearranged my office. That didn't help. Vacation was approaching. That would surely help. I planned to visit our daughter, Korey, who was studying abroad in France for a year. I should've been going bananas over this trip of a lifetime. But I was not. This wasn't right and it definitely wasn't me! I love traveling and I wanted to see our daughter.

I rearranged my office again, because it must still be the furniture's fault, right? I butted the desk up against the wall, sat down, and stared at the wall. Then I had an epiphany.

"I have literally and figuratively hit the wall!"

Things became crystal clear and I needed a change. This environment was toxic. That evening, I drafted my escape plan and explained it to Jeff. He suggested patience, "You'll outlast Roxie. People like that steamroll others and move on."

He was usually right, but I didn't have the desire or energy to wait. Thankfully my request to move to a different department was approved to occur after I returned from vacation. Woohoo!

"You cannot change the people around you, but you can change the people you choose to be around."

—Unknown

The impending change improved my outlook and would enable me to enjoy my trip. I returned from vacation energized for my position change. Jeff warned me about that "greener grass" over there, but no blade of grass was as toxic as what I'd endured! What I learned is that when mental wellness suffers, we must give it a higher priority. I reassessed the situation and took the leap!

Toxilogue: *(My book, my word.) It's like an epilogue. Wraps up the end of a toxic situation.*

My successor worked well with Roxie. Their ages and personalities were compatible. Roxie and I were like a pair of mismatched socks. Hers were double-reinforced from toe to heel with unprecedented durability. Mine were well-worn, fuzzy fleece. Our differences were complicated, but I tried to make it work. I did. I mean, I'm a fairly happy girl. Working in this environment did *not* make me a happy girl. Our best intentions aren't often enough to offset personality or other differences. And sometimes the disconnect with people is due to our own insecurities about what's in our head.

"People change, but seldom."

—unknown

The next story is from someone who wishes to remain anonymous. The names and organization have been changed to protect the non-toxic character.

"When the Workplace Isn't Working"

My gossiping coworker, Carlene, had a negative spin on most things. It always left me in a funk about the daily work and overall purpose of my role, rather than motivated and uplifted. We were supposed to work closely on a small team; it was an unavoidable situation. In addition, Carlene held onto a power differential as the seasoned veteran. She was convinced that she knew more than anyone else in the organization. (Now, *that's* confidence…but not always.) A select few acknowledged her know-it-all dynamic, which I found to be extremely toxic.

Once I came to understand that the work wasn't terrible, my other coworkers weren't all out to get each other, and that Carlene thrived on chaos, I realized I needed to change something.

I've learned over time that my laid back personality can attract strong personalities, so I changed my routine. First, I started bringing my own coffee. It was a small sign of independence. From the day I started, she had tried to create this codependent coffee thing. Every single morning, she always showed up first and handed me one of two coffees from her favorite coffee stand.

"This coffee is the BEST!" she said. I became indifferent.

Second, I closed my office door, claiming increasing work stress. I blamed it on my difficulty to focus on work tasks—which was true. Third, I claimed that I didn't work as quickly as she did. This stroked her ego to soften the blow of the closed door and coffee refusal.

She had put me in a one-down position and I used it to my advantage. This is why I knew I needed to change work habits.

In these small but substantial ways, I figured out how to move her from the front view to the sideline. I needed to create a work life in a way that worked for me. This allowed me to return to my more naturally positive self. I also reminded myself of the big picture focus: she was hindering me as an employee, which could further interfere with my professional goals. I could now stay more focused on my goals and more true to my own personality, while shutting down her attempts to pull me into gossip and negativity.

A couple years later, she moved companies. I still took her phone calls and texts. For some reason, Carlene *still* had this hold on me. I think I felt a sense of obligation and didn't want her to get upset, in the way I knew she could!

Finally, enough time passed, making it easier to space out return phone calls. We had one last lunch date. There wasn't one reason to spend my time and energy on a relationship that I didn't want to nurture.

- **Set early boundaries and protect those boundaries if needed.**
- **Pay attention: negative or chaos-loving people trip your alarm.**

—Anne Vahle, LCPC, MSEd

Time continues to pass. The occasional grocery store interaction is quite manageable with surface-level catching up and kind regards. Enough memories surface, reminding me why I chose to not continue this relationship. I simply don't have time for that, so I keep my walls up.

Here are a few of my walls for the above situation:

- no lunches
- no social media engagements
- no phone exchanges
- no empty promises of getting together to catch up

I am a different person now when it comes to toxic people and places. I just don't care to spend my time and energy caring. It only serves to complicate everything else.

"A Treat Goes Toxic"

My mammogram is always January 13th? Why is that? It's the same date our vacuum was scheduled for annual maintenance at Sears. It's easier to remember that way. The only parallel between the two things is this: both appointments suck, but that's not the point. If you've never had a mammogram, it's an awkward experience. You won't get the results immediately, but there's still a sense of completion. An annual task gets checked off for another year unless the mammogram is problematic. (I always say a quick prayer before the procedure.)

My reward for completing the mammogram was a Starbucks fix. I drove up to wait. Someone behind me honked. Maybe she recognized my car. I waved. Another honk. She'd probably hit the horn while applying lipstick. I've done that. What happened next was startling. She exited her Ford Expedition and stomped towards me.

"Oh, nice!" I thought. "She probably wants to chat to kill time."

I was wrong. She did not. She knocked heavily on my window for me to lower it.

"YOU CUT!" she said brusquely.

"I did?" I asked innocently.

Angrier yet, she said, "YEAH, YOU CUT! See all of those cars lined up out there in the alley? They're waiting to turn in here and you drove right around them and cut in line. Mmm-hmmm."

"I'm sorry. I didn't mean to," I said.

I was mortified because I'd been clueless about the process. She could've been a little nicer. I secretly decided to name her Toxic Trixie. Trixie stomped back to her car, got in and slammed the door. Nobody was going to push Trixie around!

"What can we get started for you today?" the barista asked.

"Nothing, thanks. I just got yelled at. I'll just pull out of here," I explained.

Except you can't pull out at our Starbucks. It's curbed all the way around. I feared Toxic Trixie might rear-end me before I reached the window!

Barista, "Ma'am, you can have something if you really want to."

"No thanks, but here's ten bucks. Put it towards ," I said, pointing to Trixie, "And please tell her I'm sorry. I didn't mean to cut!"

I paid, pulled away, and glanced in my rearview mirror.

You may be thinking, "That was so nice of you, Bobbe. Way to be the bigger person!"

But do you know what I was *really* thinking? **"I HOPE SHE BURNS HER TONGUE!"**

Sorry, not sorry.

Remember that toxic people can pop up at any place and at any time. We may not even know them. Also remember that you *always* have choices: flight or fight. I chose flight. Fighting was pointless. Save your sanity. Don't be dumb.

You have two basic choices:
1. *Stay around toxic people and be miserable.*
2. *Move right along.*

Ask yourself these questions:
- Will I be happier away from the toxicity? *Probably.*
- Will I miss out on some fun? *Maybe.*
- Will others follow my lead and leave the group? *Doubtfully.*
- Who cares, if it's not working for me? *Exactly!*
- Is being alone sometimes healthier? *Yes, it can be.*

"Learn to be okay with not being invited, included, or considered. Sometimes it's God's way of protection!"

—Pastor Tyrone Odums

Some telephone calls are toxic because the callers are toxic. When you can't get a word in sideways, edgewise, or otherwise the experience feels frustrating or maddening. If you've ever felt like you've been held hostage by phone, help is here. Keep reading.

Caller I.D.s: there are some we'd rather not see. If the caller I.D. name makes you cringe, it's okay to not pick up. Be like Elsa, from Disney's *"Frozen"* movie, and *"Let it Gooooooo!"* to voicemail.

If the caller doesn't leave voicemail, assume the call wasn't important. You decide if and when to return the call. It puts you in the driver's seat. This allows you time for mental preparation. Be proactive, not reactive, unless it's an emergency. I know, I know, with some people, *everything's* an emergency.

Did you pick up the call but don't have time to give it your all? Try these responses:

- "This isn't a good time to talk. I'll call you back."
- "I wish I could talk, but I can't right now."
- "Gotta run. I'm already late! Call me back and leave me a voicemail or send a text."
- "I'll have to call you back. I have a _____ (client, customer, victim, patient, or etc.)"
- "Someone's at the door! I'll call you back later."

This next story is an example of how the toxic person can even be ourselves.

My Friday Fatigue

Whooooo's a night owl? Not me, that's for sure. For years, I played cards on one Thursday night a month. Good times, friends, food all for the low, low price of $1.00 per month. But after an evening full of so much goodness, I could never fall asleep. The next work day at the bank, I always felt tired and cranky. I secretly named myself, "Cranky Banky Bobbe." I did the math:

One Cranky Banky Bobbe/per month

x Twelve months

Twelve Cranky Banky Bobbe Fridays/per year.

That's a lot of crankiness! Also, Fridays were busier and longer work days, too. The Thursday night fun didn't offset the Friday fatigue. I decided that the personal and professional cost of cranky Fridays was too high and became a substitute instead of a regular player. Family members and coworkers were most grateful for this. When we realize the toxic person is us, it's time to examine what needs correcting. Nobody wants to be that person!

st**R**ess no evil

REST

We tend to resist rest rather than forfeit precious time in our day. Think of rest as a productive activity. It doesn't need to last seven or eight hours a night. Eight hours is great, but not always attainable. The Greater Good Science Center at Berkeley advises, "Even a short, twenty minute nap can boost your ability to concentrate by giving your brain a chance to restore depleted energy. The most obvious napping benefit is that it increases alertness and decreases fatigue."

Ways to rest. It all counts. It all helps.

- **Nap** when you can. Noon yoga class ended in the dark with quiet music for five minutes. I fell asleep instantly. (I'm fortunate to be a swift snoozer.)

- **Connect** with art and nature and **disconnect** for some electronic free time.

- **Alone time** in your home or anywhere

- **Walk** outside briefly to take a break for mental rest and reset.

- **Be free from busy-ness** and do nothing for a bit. It's one of the best things you can do!

- **Meditate.** Here are a few recommended apps: UCLA Mindful Awareness Research Center @UCLA.MARC, Calm, Insight Meter, My Life (formerly Breathe), and Delmora.

- **Rest can be as simple** as watching reruns of *Schitt's Creek*, NCIS, or Friends.

Remember that rest is a productive activity, yielding positive results. Don't underestimate the value of rest. Duration is not the key to beneficial rest. It's okay to rest without any guilt. There are no trophies for those who claim to be the most tired.

"If you feel like you need a break then take one. There isn't anything productive about burning yourself out."

—Simply Sophie Designs

str**E**ss no evil

EXERCISE

Exercise your options: Part 1, Mental Fitness
I'll bet you expected another yawny lecture about making exercise a high priority. First, let's take a little zig and zag over to another fitness area that deserves attention: mental fitness.

Counseling or therapy are both valuable options to managing serious stress. The other tips in this book are of a less serious nature, but as I learned about the growing number of individuals who suffer from severe stress, a section addressing these prevalent issues only made sense.

"Yes, it's hard to make that first call. Yes, it's embarrassing to admit the mental struggle is real. Still, each time I've surrendered my ego and accepted reality, that one phone call improved my life exponentially! When you find a good fit with a professional, you'll be heard and helped effectively."

—Bobbe White, CLL-E, NOCW

What if I don't have a good fit with my mental health professional? Anne Vahle, MSEd, LCPC, urges you, "Mention it. Make sure he or she is clear about your needs and expectations. It might be beneficial for your personal progress and is great practice for speaking your mind. If that fails, or you're uncomfortable speaking up, then move right along!" Consider other types of service from businesses. When we don't like the product or service, we speak up or move along.

"You always have options."
—Shirley Longlett, LCPC-retired

Getting good help has gotten easier! Counseling and therapy are multi-deliverable, not only face-to-face. Search, "Find a therapist" at psychologytoday.com. There are filters for payment options, locations, and specialties. Professionally staffed platforms like Teledoc, MDLive, BetterHelp, and Talkspace are also accessible by multiple means. Here's a virtual fist-bump to the evolution of technology!

Stress is a catch-all concept. Anne Vahle, MSEd, LCPC, reminds us, "Stress is a fairly general label or a catch-all idea. As a professional," Vahle says, "I will start there, knowing full well that there is an underlying emotion causing the person's stress, such as anxiety, fear, anger, or excitement. People may struggle to name the real emotion when in an emotional mindset.

"All stress is rooted in a basic emotion,"

—Anne Vahle, MSEd, LCPC

To make progress, the primary emotion causing stress must be identified. Many scholars studied the primary emotions. Robert Plutchik, PhD, proposed eight emotions. He designed the wheel of primary, secondary, and tertiary emotions (AKA Feelings Wheel.) Dr. Paul Eckman, identified six emotions. The Chinese ancient "Book of Rites" (circa 1st century BC) defined seven. The precise number is subjective, so I chose Plutchik, because I like to say his name. (I bet you just said it too, didn't you?) I took liberty with his flower petal model in order to align with my book theme.

Vahle continues, "A mental health professional can be helpful, because our emotions can be quite confusing! Understanding your emotions will provide a simple and logical way to make sense of the feeling that is fueling your stress. Until pinpointed, it's difficult to reduce or eliminate the body's responses, (e.g. muscle tension, headache, fatigue, crying, weight loss/gain, elevated blood pressure, depression, or anxiety.)"

"What mental health needs is more sunlight, more candor, more unashamed conversation."

—Glenn Close, Actress

Could mental health gyms be the next big deal? A mental health gym is a safe place created for the purpose of talking about tough mental health topics. Coa is a new venture that bills itself as the world's first mental health gym. Coa is short for coalesce, which means growing together.

Coa co-founder and CEO, Alexa Meyer, noticed that San Francisco had physical fitness gyms on every corner, but no visible options for emotional health. This is how mental health has been handled for decades—out of sight and under the radar.

Cleveland Cavaliers Forward, Kevin Love, is an investor of Coa. Throughout his stellar career, Kevin suffered from severe social anxiety and depression. Few knew of his mental health issues prior to 2017, when he had a panic attack during an NBA game. Michael Phelps, Olympic swimming phenom, began talking about his depression in 2020. HBO produced the documentary, "Weight of Gold," where Phelps shared his experiences and struggles during and after achieving world class excellence.

When notable people speak out about their illnesses, it can move others to action. Coa has established mental health pop-up gyms in larger cities. The organization provided an online presence when efforts were interrupted by COVID-19. Coa hopes to build brick and mortar centers soon. Visit their website at www.joincoa. com.

Stress gets a bad rap. Not all stress is negative. Emotions can cause eustress (i.e. good stress) in addition to distress (bad stress.) Distress can trigger ineffective or uncomfortable feelings or behavior, but be aware that both types of stress can sharpen our focus and raise our energy levels. In this way, distress can be a positive motivator for a person to take action, make changes, or adjustments. Either way, adrenaline provides the extra oomph.

People always asked me before a swimming or speaking event, "Are you nervous?"

My answer would always be, "Yes, but in a *good* way!"

Good stress floods our bodies with endorphins (the feel-good hormones) and adrenaline. Awareness and positive expectancy is heightened. Fill me up, Buttercup!

<u>E</u>xercise your options: Part 2, physical fitness

"The best fitness is the one you are going to do."

—Dr. Colleen Hacker,
Women's National Team's Mental Skills Coach

This section is brief because there's little I can add to what you already know. We know why, when, how, what, and where to exercise. Why, then, do some of us still not get enough—or any—exercise? Someone justified their resistance to exercise this way:

"But if I start exercising, I can never stop!"

That's right. Exercise is not a temporary or cumulative plan. It's a lifestyle, habit, and a commitment. But, if years and years of exercise sounds torturous, try thinking of it as a regular vitamin. Like vitamins, workouts are only good for that day, every other day, or whatever your routine is. Then you do it again.

Every time I go to exercise, it takes discipline to overcome resistance. Whenever you move past the resistance, you'll think, "I'm so glad I did it!"

"Not once have I ever said that I couldn't wait to go work out, but afterwards, I am always so glad that I made myself."

—MaryBeth McGee, RN, MS

Overcome resistance by adopting these tenets for successful exercise:

- Do something you enjoy.
- Move something regularly.
- Avoid boredom. Change-up your workout periodically.
- Jump out of your jammies and into your workout clothes when it's the first thing on your schedule. Have your gym bag packed when exercising later that day.
- It's never too late to start!

"The best time to workout is the time when you will actually do it."

—Bobbe White, CLL-E, NOCW

Daily, regular movement of some sort is the key. After one presentation, an elderly gentleman approached me and said, "I totally agree with your philosophy to move something regularly and I want to tell you that I have a movement regularly. Every single day. And I feel great!" He had taken my suggestion in a different direction!

I said, "That's great, Sir! It's not the kind of movement I was talking about, but hey, keep going!"

Be like the postal service "Nor wind, nor sleet, nor rain, nor cold..." Outside activity must be continual to help us acclimate to seasonal weather changes. Otherwise, we are apt to skip it.

Do you feel nervous going to a gym because everyone will stare at you? And it won't be because they're in awe of you. R-E-L-A-X! Gym enthusiasts have more concern for themselves than for you. In fact, many times, I almost feel as if I'm invisible when athletes are there. Trust me on this one. They really could care less— as long as I'm not hogging the equipment they want to use!

If you can't, don't or won't go to a gym, consider investing in basic equipment or online programs. Buy hand weights, stretch bands, or a yoga mat. Just do something!

50 REASONS TO EXERCISE
by Darebee (darebee.com)

1. lifts your mood
2. strengthens your heart
3. improves posture
4. improves learning abilities
5. builds self-esteem
6. keeps your brain fit
7. keeps your body fit and able
8. boosts mental health
9. reduces stress
10. makes you feel happier
11. has anti-aging effects
12. boosts your immune system
13. improves skin tone and color
14. improves sleeping patterns
15. helps prevent strokes
16. improves joint function
17. improves muscle strength
18. alleviates anxiety
19. sharpens memory
20. boosts productivity
21. helps to control addictions
22. boosts creative thinking
23. improves body image
24. gives you confidence
25. helps you keep focused in life
26. strengthens your bones
27. improves eating habits
28. increases longevity
29. prevents colds
30. improves appetite
31. improves cholesterol levels
32. lessens (certain) kinds of cancer
33. lowers high blood pressure
34. lowers risk of dementia
35. lowers risk of diabetes
36. eases back pain
37. decreases osteoporosis risk
38. lessens feelings of depression
39. prevents muscle loss
40. increases energy and endurance
41. increases sports performance
42. increases pain resistance
43. improves balance and coordination
44. improves oxygen supply to cells
45. improves concentration
46. helps with self control
47. lessens fatigue
48. helps foster fitness friends/ community*
49. makes life more exciting
50. improves quality of life

*Darebee had a duplicate benefit listed, so I replaced it with a benefit of my choice.

stre**S**s no evil

This is the other two-for-one tip:
one letter with two options

SOLO AND SOCIAL

SOLO

My wise and wonderful mother-in-law, Lisetta, once gave me the following advice. "If you wait for Jeff to do everything with you, you're going to miss a lot." Initially, I dismissed her advice. Wasn't every spouse like my dad? He went everywhere willingly with Mom. There was never a fight, any resistance, or discussion over attending any event. He didn't whine or pout. He'd only ever ask Mom two things:

- "What should I wear?"
- "What time do we need to leave?"

At this point in life, Lisetta clearly knew her son better than I did. It's that acorn-falling-from- the-tree idea. I first got a taste of what missing out felt like a few years before we got married. The Jethro Tull Band was coming to our Illinois State campus, circa 1975. I know every word to two of Tull's albums: Aqualung and Thick as a Brick. I'm not kidding. Jeff didn't know Aqualung from an iron lung. He had zero interest in going. I accepted his disinterest and tried to squelch my desire to attend.

Wouldn't you know it? Jeff's buddies had an extra ticket and asked him to go. And he went. Yes, he did! I pouted all weekend. Actually, I pouted for twenty-four years until I *finally* saw Jethro Tull in 1999. That's a long time to pout. Some of you are thinking, "Yeah, I'd be mad too!" Others of you are thinking, "Who in the hell is Jethro Tull?" (It's a seventies thing!)

Ian Anderson, master flutist of Jethro Tull Band.

I vowed this would *not* happen again! As a result, I'm pleased to report that many potential fights between us have been avoided. Now, if it's mutually agreeable—which it usually is—I'll go anyway. I don't always like it, but it's better than the alternative.

What does this have to do with this solo/social tip? Whenever I want to attend an event and Jeff declines, I'll ask someone to go with me. If that fails, I may choose to roll solo, rather than miss the event all together.

Rolling solo hasn't always been comfortable, but it became easier over time. It can for you too. Do you currently struggle with the idea of going somewhere alone? Do you find it stressful to shop, walk, or dine alone? Can you travel by car, train, or plane alone? If not, this tip is for you!

"Don't go alone out of spite. Go if it's important to you to go."

—Bobbe White, CLL-E, NOCW

Many activities are more fun with two or more people, but sometimes it just doesn't work out that way. Mom would argue that, when going alone, my life was at stake. She fully embraced the buddy system. Admittingly, there are times when it's foolish to go alone, but with a bit of street smarts, most risks can be reduced.

If going places alone causes stress, can it also be a tip to relieve stress? So glad you asked! It's not completely easy. Going solo can definitely be uncomfortable at first. With practice, your awkwardness will lessen. It gets easier. In the end, you'll have reduced a source of your stress. Sometimes it becomes necessary to go somewhere alone. By practicing, you'll be appreciative of your acquired skill.

"Learn to go places by yourself. It fosters self-confidence and reduces stress. Self-satisfaction and calmness increase too. You'll sound like a proud five-year-old, "I did it all by myself!" Pride is a pretty great benefit.

—Bobbe White, CLL-E, NOCW

We all have different interests. Begging someone to accompany us rarely works well, *especially* if it's a significant other, who has little to no interest in the event. Pre-event grumbling and fussing sucks the fun right out of going. The unhappy attendee may also be resistant to acting or looking cordial, or not be willing to stay long. We're all just different and must be willing to compromise sometimes. I don't always release Jeff, but I do weigh each situation. Below are some of our compromises:

- **Annual workplace parties** were required of Jeff every five years. (I received a five year award.) My fortieth year was 2020, which called for his attendance. Covid canceled the party and all I can say is, "Jeff's a lucky duck."

- **School Reunions** aren't required. He went to my high school reunion once. Never again.

- **Weddings/funerals** are predominantly solo for me, unless it's family or a mutual friend.

"Controlling people takes away another person's power, which creates an unsafe situation. The suggestions here are for people who are looking to compromise and work together, with the end goal of lowering both people's stress levels."

—Anne Vahle, LCPC, MSEd

This approach works for Jeff and me. Every relationship is unique. However, if learning to go alone somewhere is stressful for you and you'd like to improve, keep reading.

How to enter a room in two easy steps:

1. Inhale. (Don't forget to exhale too!) Breathing deeply helps calm your body.

2. Walk in. Grand entrances are not required. (But they can be fun!) Try to imagine walking in like you own the place. Ladies stop hugging your purses to death! You're too old for a security blanket. Aren't you? You are strong and confident. You can do this!

One woman I know says a mantra whenever entering a room feeling awkward. She repeats to herself, "I look GOOOOOOD in my dress!" If you can say it—if only in your mind—you can believe it. Own it! Our minds are powerful tools when it comes to self-messaging.

"If it's mentionable—even to yourself— it's manageable!"

—Bobbe White

He said what??? I once worked for Jerry, a goofy photographer, in Ohio. Before taking any pictures, he always said the same thing to every woman. It was inappropriate back in 1978. Can you even imagine this happening today?

Jerry, "Okay, knockers up!"

Women cringed every time he said it. So did I.

When Jerry took my passport photo, he said, "Knockers Up!" I hate to admit it, but I did sit up a bit taller. Darn him. The photographer understood that better posture conveys confidence. He just didn't have a lot of tact when conveying his message.

It's the same principle, when entering a room: stand up taller, put one foot before the other, and repeat. Before long, you're in! To be less offensive, you can come up with your own reminder, besides "knockers up." Shorten it to K.U. or say, "Sit up and look regal, Girl!"

I'm in. Now what? Find a seat at a table or in a row. Ask, "Is anyone sitting here?" If it's not being saved, it's yours! And yay you! You did it! Reminder: as a COVID precaution, chairs may be empty to maintain social distancing.

Networking 101

This sure sounds like networking advice. Good catch! It kind of is. There are parallels between getting comfortable being by yourself in both personal and professional situations. Self-confidence empowers you to be more effective in your business obligations and to feel less nervous and self-conscious in the process.

Feeling awkward?

- Head for the food or the bar. I know people who would go hungry before approaching the buffet table alone. Either one provides you with a destination and a mission. Bartenders are cordial, whether you order vodka or V-8 juice. Why? Hellooooo, tips!

- Compliment the wait staff when they replenish food, bring you a new fork, or dessert. Say something simple, like, "It looks good!" or "Thanks for bringing the _____." Hey, at least you're talking to somebody, right? Engage others in conversation. It's a good way to become memorable in someone else's eyes, especially when you're appreciative And that may well as be you!

- Directional anxiety keeps some people from asking directions, such as to the restroom. They'd rather not ask and then hold it until they practically wet their pants! Is this you? If so, remember that hotel or conference staff, security guards, or ushers have answered this question a bazillion times. It doesn't require a conversation. Watch this:

You: "Restrooms?"

Staff: "Down the hall, on your right."

You: "Thanks."

Staff: "My pleasure."

The end. Ta-Dah! You did it!

Additional tips for dining solo:

"Date yourself—shower yourself with love.

—Andrea Copenhaver, Executive Director

- **Where and what to eat** are often the first decisions to make—particularly in new cities. Calm apprehension with some advanced research. Hotel registration staff answer these questions frequently. Big city hotels typically have concierge desks. (Tip: tip the concierge!) Or ask a friend or business contact for suggestions.

- **Table, booth, or bar?** I have found there are usually tables for one in most places. I have found the staff to be welcoming when I'm a party of one. Consider eating at the bar, particularly in busy airports—as long as you can safely climb on and off the stool.

- **You choose.** When alone, I love the freedom of picking the restaurant, bar, museum without discussion, compromise, or argument. My guilty pleasure is eating at the top of the city's tallest building. Make a reservation and request window seating. (Afraid of heights? Skip this tip!)

- **Request a window** seat on *any* floor. It provides something to look at besides your phone. People-watching out a window can be very entertaining. Gaze away! We clutch our phones like some people clutch their purses. Put that phone down and those knockers up! (Did I just say that? I seriously need to find a better alternative *soon*.)

- **How many?** When the maître d' or hostess asks, "How many?" Don't say, "Just one." Drop the word *just* like an old high school girlfriend or boyfriend! Saying, "Just one," trivializes you. Say, "One for dinner." Then proudly follow the host to your seat.

"Being alone does not render you insignificant! Don't play small!"

—Bobbe White, CLL-E, NOCW

Be present when dining solo. Try hard to resist technology. It can be awkward sitting alone. Focus on the positive. Soak up the view if you snagged that window seat. Savor your drink.

Taste your food. SLOW DOWN. Scan the restaurant casually to feel the vibe. Notice the hustle of the wait staff. A quick exchange with the hostess or staff can make you feel more comfortable.

My friend, Lisa, always arrived at lunch early. She read a book until I arrived. Reading made her look very self-confident. It's hard to explain, but somehow the book seemed different from being engaged with technology. Added bonus: someone sees your book and it triggers a conversation.

Grab pen and paper; write about your experience as it's unfolding, or make your grocery list.

"Alone doesn't mean lonely."

—Penni Ippensen, LCSW Therapist

My experience with rolling solo:

- **Broadway for one**. My family gave me a one season ticket to the St. Louis Fox Broadway series. It's weird, right? Here's my theory: when the lights go down and the curtain goes up, nobody knows if you're alone or not. Sometimes I'll go with a friend, but for other shows, I go alone.

- **Solitary travel can be challenging.** My family laughs at my navigational ability. Ironically, when alone, I travel just fine by myself, whether traveling by plane, train, or automobile. Sure, I've made wrong turns. I've had close boarding calls. Who hasn't? Thanks to Siri and my phone alarm, I've only missed one connection in twenty years.

- I attended a **conference** in 2017. Rolling solo, older and grayer than 97% of the attendees sent my awkwardness level up a flagpole! At the start, we learned the conference rule: "Nobody lets another person stand alone." Everyone quickly connected. My comfort level improved, my confidence increased, and I was more open to learning.

When in Rome

Actually, we were in Paris, not Rome. On New Year's Eve, Korey, friends, and I congregated with a million others to see the Eiffel Tower's light show. After the midnight crescendo, Korey and company went clubbing. She gave me explicit directions to get home by way of the Metro, Paris' rapid transit system.

My plans became worthless. Authorities had rerouted revelers to get them out of the city after midnight. Police and dogs were posted throughout the stations. The natives were easily spotted, as they calmly reconfigured their routes. We tourists, on the other hand, were completely discombobulated. My foreign navigational skills are mediocre, at best, but fortunately, adrenaline kicked in and instantly honed my ability and alertness.

On one leg of the route, several of us stood on seats to avoid the train floor. New Year's in Paris is like anywhere in the world. People party and drink more. Some lose their cookies on the train floor. It was gaggy at best.

At another stop, I studied the wall map. Two women asked me for help with the schedule revisions. Yes, you read that right, "THEY ASKED ME!" They figured that a middle-aged, white-haired woman, wearing a trench coat, who was riding the subway during the middle of the night would likely be Parisian. Hardly! Amazingly, I was able to redirect them. TA DAH!

By 3:30 a.m., I'd been recalculating routes for hours. My final stop was closed. The closest I could get to our apartment was the stop before mine. Right before me stood a Holiday Inn. If all else failed, the desk crew would likely speak English. Maybe they would grant me a seat on their sofa until daybreak. I asked for directions to our apartment. For crêpe's sake, I was only one block away! Getting to my destination after traveling Paris all night—with rusty French—is what I call a "Godwink." I called Nick at 4:00 a.m. It was 9:00 p.m. Chicago time.

"Mom, why are you up at 4:00 a.m.?" Nick asked. I explained my adventure in more detail than I'm sure he wanted.

"Were you scared?" he asked.

"A little. Then I had to figure it out. People were very helpful—the ones that I could understand anyway. I even helped some lost Americans. They thought I was a native. How crazy is that?"

"That's pretty crazy!" Nick agreed.

I'm happy to say that's the last time I've rolled solo all night long, but it's not the last time I've gotten lost. Cheers to New Years!

SOCIAL

Connecting with others seems easy—unless you're an introvert. Like some species of animals, we're raised in packs, otherwise known as families. Occasionally in high school, Mom would find me in a dim room, feet propped up, listening to Pink Floyd, Led Zeppelin, or Black Sabbath. Sounds kind of dark, right?

"Why don't you call some friends?" Mom would ask.

"I don't know, Mom, because sometimes I don't feel like being with people." Sure, I still have those days, every once in a while, but I've since learned that I need connection for wellness. It's complicated. Above, we discussed how it can be healthy, even enjoyable, to be alone. But other times when we're alone we may need people. Anne Vahle, LCPC reminds us, "Being alone and being lonely are different and that is important here. The exception is to not seek out someone who is toxic to you, in which case, you'll want to cut and run."

"Push past the discomfort of the moment in order to connect with others."

—Anne Vahle, LCPC, MSEd

Finding humans:

1. Start with family, if they're accessible and available.

2. Go outside. Be neighborly. Find a yard sale (You don't have to buy anything.)

3. Go to cafés and diners. Reminder: smile! Many solo patrons go to cafés just to hangout.

4. Walk the dog. Head for a dog park. Pet connection often fosters human connection.

5. Find a free community program of interest. Conversation starts with a common interest.

6. Volunteer for a cause. Rarely will organizations turn you away.

7. Mentor a student. He or she may be lonely too. Win-win.

Finding people is the first step. Talking to them is the second step. Just because you don't speak to anyone in the coffee shop doesn't mean it's unhelpful. Closed-mouthed smiles and head nods can go a long way in feeling part of the community. In this case, it's a community of coffee drinkers who are digging the peace and quiet!

stres**S** no evil

SCRUB

I know you know what scrub means. I looked it up for more insight.

Scrub: to clean or remove with hard rubbing. Synonyms include scour, rub, cancel, or eliminate." (merriam-webster.com)

Whether it's the sink, the garage, or yourself, scrubbing can make us feel better. The act of scrubbing—or cleaning—brings the added benefit of exercise. Plus, scrubbing windows and floors burns calories and endorphins (There are those crazy endorphins again!) Scrubbing helps you blow off steam too. In my poll results found at the end of the book, several responders said cleaning was their activity of choice to minimize stress. It's not my drug of choice, but perhaps I should reconsider.

"Anticipate the act of scrubbing as you start your shower. Apply soap to your washcloth and/or your hair. Enjoy the soap scent. Feel the water hit your body and remove all of the bad toxins. Let things go that no longer serve you—literally and figuratively— down the drain. Your skin and your soul are left feeling invigorated. Your body is clean and fresh."

—Andrea Copenhaver, Executive Director

For some, scrubbing is tied to drudgery rather than stress relief. In that case, consider activities *besides* housecleaning that are enjoyable to scrub. (i.e. your face, body, children, the car, or the dog.) It's an activity with both physical and mental benefits. Get creative. Think of the object you're washing as a way to rid yourself of sweat, dirt, the day or certain issues away.

S. C. Johnson & Son invented Scrubbing Bubbles®. They combined the scrubbing effort with the whimsical nature of bubbles. This is a great duo! What is it about bubbles? They are simply magical, that's what! Perhaps it's because bubbles can float in air and water, they're colorful, clear, and even effervescent. Try the following ideas below to watch your stress bubble away!

- **Bathtub**: scrub yourself (but not with Scrubbing Bubbles®!) or lounge in a bubble bath until you get interrupted. Count on dogs or small children to need your attention the minute that you step into the tub. Save the bubble bath until the littles go to bed.

- **Scrub dishes** in oodles of bubbles. It's more enjoyable and will seem less like a chore. Make the task a team effort and include others (i.e. partner, teens, grandkids.)

- **Blow bubbles.** Feel silly? Buy two bottles and give one to a child. Double the bubbles with a bubble buddy! Our neighbors set up a bubble machine in their driveway. A sign nearby read: "Think happy!" People who walked, biked, or drove by responded with a wave, smile, or a honk.

- **Car washes** turned my kids and me into frequent fliers! It was the best bubble-therapy as the ribbons, flaps, bubbles and water cleaned the car. With or without passengers, I still hit the car wash. Bubbles are relaxing. Amanda, my former co-worker, heads for the car wash before work, to level off a tough morning, because it works. Man, I was so jealous when she got a monthly car wash membership for Christmas!

    If you have room at home, wash the car there. Spraying your helpers— weather permitting— can be a fun fight. Expect immediate retaliation!

- **Scrub your windows at home**—inside and out—for a better view. Let the light shine in your life. (Hint: vinegar and water are a simple combo to complete the job.)

"I wish bubbles could be a forecast."

—WTForecast

stress <u>N</u>o evil

<u>N</u>O

No. NO! No? Nope! Nah. Huh uh. No way! Nooooooooooo! How can two little letters cause so much stress? It's because many people struggle to say, "No." Sometimes we even say, "Yes," when we mean no.

Try these two rhymes to help anchor your decisions:
—Don't say, "Yes" if you can't give it your best!
—The wrong yes will give you stress.
—Bobbe White, CLL-E, NOCW

Last year, at a fundraiser, friends bid on a vacation. I offered to be a substitute if spots opened up and before too long, they did. My answer was, "YES!" before I did the math. It'd be pricier than I realized. Truthfully, I hadn't given much thought to the cost. It wasn't terribly expensive for a week's vacation at a beautiful place in a fabulous destination, but it might mean forfeiting another trip I'd planned. That dreaded feeling grew in my gut. Then I knew I should've said, "No."

It was awkward and embarrassing to regret the offer after showing interest, but soon after reversing my answer, my stress subsided.

"It's okay to change your yes to a no, if you know deep inside that no is the better option for you."
—Andrea Copenhaver, Executive Director

In an excerpt from her book, "It's Your Business," Christine Cashen, hall of fame speaker and author, reminds us to protect our priorities. "Here's the skinny—we only have so many hours in the day and we usually sacrifice time on what really matters for time spent doing a bunch of insignificant things that really don't. Most of us are not victims; we're volunteers!"

Ways to say, "No:"

- **"No."** Boom! Just like that. Too harsh? Read on.

- **"I can't."** You didn't even have to use the "no" word.

- **"Let me check and get back to you."** Buy some time if you cannot think fast.

- **"No. It's a *lonnnnnng* story."** Trust me, *nobody* wants to hear your long story.

- **"In this season of my life**, any "yes" I say to you is a "no" that I have to say to my _____ (partner, children, parents, dog, etc.)" Who can argue with those priorities?

- **"OOOPS* Is that what I said? That's not what I meant!"** (AKA the flip-flop or backpedal.) Hey, it seems to work for politicians. You see, what Bobbe *MEANT* to say was, "Yes, it's definitely no on your request." Or was it? Hmmmmm.

Avoid saying, "No, because." The reason is irrelevant whether you have to go to _____ (the doctor, the grocery, or Tahiti.) Why? *Nobody* wants to hear your becauses. I can't because I have a haircut, a meeting, or a colonoscopy. The person asking really doesn't care about the reason. You'll basically sound like Charlie Brown's teacher, "No, because wah-wah- wah-wah-wah-wah-wah-wah." Save your becauses.

"Anything that you say after 'because' is bullshit."
—Dax Shepard's podcast, The Armchair Expert

*OOOPS stands for **O**verwhelmed, **O**verworked, **O**vercommitted, **P**owerless, and **S**tressed, which is what you will feel when you say "yes" and mean "no."

Why we say yes when we mean no:

- Brain freeze occurs when we're caught off guard, "Yes," slips out!

- We don't want to disappoint.

- We try to avoid conflicts.

- We feel guilty when we regret.

- We feel obligated, believing something is expected of us.

- We are insecure. "But my brownies are better than *everybody's*. I'll stay up all night to accommodate, even if it exhausts me!" Over-giving can be annoying and self-defeating.

- We get bullied into saying, "yes". Be your own advocate and control your agenda.

- We are used to always saying, "Yes." In other words, it's a natural habit.

"Just because you can, doesn't mean you have to."

—Shirley Longlett, M.S., LCPC (Retired)

stress n**O** evil

<u>O</u>UTDOORS

"There's a reason they call it the great outdoors. You've never heard anyone call it the mediocre outdoors, have you?"

—David Glickman, Keynote Speaker, Author

As a little boy, our son, Nick, would tug hard to open the sliding door.

"How is it out there?" I'd ask.

He always answered: "It's BIGGGGGGGGGG!"

That it is! There are so many great ways to experience the outdoors.

Going outdoors can be planned, spontaneous, ordinary or outstanding. Whether I'm hiking in the Colorado Rockies or mowing my grass in Quincy, Illinois, I get enjoyment out of both types of outdoor activities. I also enjoy bodies of water, such as a pond, lake, river, or ocean. I like water in any form—except when it's on our basement floor!

Even a few minutes outside can improve wellness. Few things are better than fresh air. Being outside eases stress by giving you a sensory rich experience of sights, sounds, colors, and movements. Remember the chapter on sound? Outside can be like a white noise app for your entire system. Get outside! Get some sky! Can't go outside? Find a window. Drink in the view.

"There's no such thing as bad weather, only bad clothing."

—Alfred Wainwright

Basic math for being dressed suitably, in any weather:

- **Cold:** add clothes, gloves, hat, and boots
- **Hot:** subtract clothes, add hat, and shades
- **Wet:** add raincoat, umbrella, and boots
- **Dark weather:** add flashlight and neon colors

"When planning trip itineraries, explore local park systems to experience something new and special to that community. Many park costs are free or minimal cost for certain hours or a day of adventure."

—Andrea Copenhaver, Executive Director

Forest bathing

Qing Li, a Nippon Medical School professor in Tokyo, studied forest bathing, which means spending time in the woods. Li measured the benefits of slowing down and becoming immersed in the natural environment. When we take time to soak it all up—scents, sounds, terrain, and foliage—there are measurable benefits listed below:

- Strengthens immunity caused by rapid response of human natural killer (NK) cells
- Reduces chance of heart attack
- Protection against obesity and diabetes
- Mood-boosting effects
- More energy, better sleep
- Decreased inflammation
- Clearer, more comfortable skin
- Soothes sore muscles
- Lungs expand, as we tend to breathe deeply to take in the scented woods and foliage.
- General improvement from illness

No forest handy? If possible, step outdoors to stand, breathe, sit, meditate, relax in the grass, observe foliage, and move about, if possible. Get the dog and the kids outside too. If you work inside all day, take your lunch outside. Consider quick and easy possible activities.

stress no <u>E</u>vil

<u>E</u>XPLORE

"Anything that focuses on what you're doing rather than on what you should be doing is a good stress reliever."

—Mayo Clinic News Network, July 15, 2019

Go ahead. Do something different. Spark some new energy with a new activity or adventure and recharge yourself! Never doubt the ability of your system to adapt to a new activity. I don't mean master it, I mean try. Give yourself a taste of something different. It helps deter the brain from what may be causing you stress.

Stress alert! Exploring may cause a new kind of stress in the process. You might feel excited or nervous about embarking upon a new activity. It's worth trying, if attempted in a friendly environment. When nervousness is holding you back, maybe it's actually excitement. Rename your emotion and go for it!

To repeat, mastery of the new activity is irrelevant here even. This can be difficult for the perfectionist personality. I'm guilty. The important thing is that you attempt a new activity and welcome its diversions. It's perfectly okay to fail, flop, or flub.

After many years, I've started golfing again. Talk about lack of mastery! It gets very frustrating when recalling that I used to be better. Then I must remember why I'm out there. Fun, friends, exercise—if walking—and fresh air.

"I want my tombstone to read, "She tried."

—Penni Ippensen, LCSW Therapist

Trying implies doing without regard for mastery of all the things. Penni experiences what life has to offer. She pushes past resistance. She lives the life she wants. What better way is there?

I Can See Clearly Now—The Fear is Gone!

After many years of sticking plastic lenses in her eyes, Christine Cashen developed an allergy to her contacts. "Lasik (surgery) sounded like the way to go, but fear always got the best of me. I researched doctors, did the pre-screen thing and had the surgery DONE (really!) within a week. (I knew that waiting and thinking would mess with my head.) So here I am a few weeks later, seeing better than ever and wondering why I didn't do this sooner."

"The whole (Lasik) experience got me thinking about how fear holds us back. But I had to deal and move forward—because I was forced to make a change. How often do we have blurred vision without knowing it? We begin to believe that the blur is normal and live with it. It usually isn't until we get out of the situation that we see things more clearly."

—Christine Cashen, Speaker Hall of Fame, Author

Writing is an easy activity to explore. It's safe too! There are no onlookers to watch or critique us. Grab paper and pen and start writing. Note the key word is *writing*, not typing. Taking pen to paper seems to yield better results. Take a keyboard break.

- Write—or print—to release pent-up emotions.

- Clinical research supports that taking a pen to paper activates the emotional part of our brain in a way typing cannot.

- Handwritten pieces can be saved or destroyed. It's your choice!

"It is about the actual act of writing, connecting with your words on a visceral level."

—Dolly Garland

59

Okay, let's write! About what? Consider these ideas:

- **Gratitude** journal is an easy starting point. Note and record a few daily incidents. You'll feel better for identifying such things. Keep it simple. Full sentences aren't required. There aren't any rules except to actually use the journal. Having a journal, or two, or three on your shelf is one thing. Actually making entries is the key.

- **Brainstorm or brain dump** your ideas, goals, and dreams even if they're crazy!

- **Bucket List**: Describe the details. Anticipation can be as rewarding as the event itself!

- **Write funny stuff down.** (e.g. funny things that you saw, heard, did, or even thought. Remember: you're not performing for an audience. The humor is for you. Focusing on funny stuff is a healthy diversion from stress.

- **Stories and poetry** can be written by any one, of any age, or level of writing experience.

- **Daily diary**: reflect on your day and tune in to your current mindset.

Uh-oh! What if someone finds what I wrote? We all worry about this when expressing pent-up emotions on paper. Writing with emotion feels quite satisfying, if I must say so myself. When writing, brutal honesty is the goal. It's personal power, but you'll want to find a safe place for your work to reflect on later. Otherwise, destroy it so your worry is gone. Friends, we're trying to reduce stress here, not create more of it for you!

Besides writing, there are gazillions of options to explore. Some of my own explorations have been successful. I completely failed at others, but at least I tried. Here is my partial list:

- **Theatre** classes. I tried beginner's acting and failed miserably! Trust me, it's harder than it looks. My tuition became a donation and my hat is off to actors and actresses. (I saw my instructor, Brandon, yesterday. He invited me back. Yikes...do I dare?

- **Art classes** offer painting, drawing, sculpting, weaving, pottery making, and more. I loved Lush & Brush with other novices, just like me. For a fair fee, the Quincy Art Center provided paint, canvas, aprons, and instruction. Our group provided food and beverages. My masterpiece hung in our gallery for weeks (i.e. garage) until it disappeared. It may have been theft, but I doubt it.

- **Drop in fitness and dance classes** help energize your current efforts. Inform instructors you're new. (They can usually tell anyway.) I've stumbled through many classes. So long as my body is moving, it's exercise.

- **Yoga, meditation, or sound therapy classes** teach gentle movement, stretching, mindfulness, and relaxation. Enhanced breathing and oxygen exchange are great side benefits.

- **Museums**, open houses, gardens, and loft tours are found in many cities. The fun is in the looking.

- **Puzzles**, including crossword, word search, jigsaw, or Sudoku, can suck you in for hours. If it's relaxing it has merit. At 95, Mom and I did word searches. Each time she found a word, she gave a little fist pump!

- **Chalk up the sidewalk or doodle on the driveway.** Artistry is not required and cleanup is easy. Just add water.

- **Coloring isn't just for kids.** Adult coloring books have come of age, or grab a children's coloring book. An easy, free option is to scribble on plain paper. If you have the urge, go ahead and just color the monkeys and the bananas in this book! When you have the opportunity, grab crayons, markers, or colored pencils and color away. Color while waiting for kids or for curbside service. Coloring calms us.

- **Crafting** includes many art forms, ranging from sculpture, to metalwork, to weaving, or painting—and all things in between. Materials can consist of virtually anything...even trash. Crafts can be functional, decorative, or fashionable. Sometimes they can even be income producing!

- **Music lessons** often allow you to choose private or group. Options are endless. Look for guitar, voice, percussion, or piano classes. Drumming therapy was quite unusual. We learned we really couldn't do it wrong!

"I checked off a bucket list item in Hawaii—on a clothing optional beach. It was total freedom and no stress!"

—Kevin Hannant, Playright

Below are two business cards I designed for my crafts. I liked finding my perfect titles, which are circled below. These titles simply tickle me. Then again, I'm easily entertained.

Above title: Head Corker   **Above title: Head Looper**

"No risk...no reward. If you are risk averse, try chanting, "Ohhhh what the heckkk, gooooo for it anywayyyyy." You'll never know the outcome if you don't try, nor are you worse off than before when you've gone another direction."

—Christine Cashen, Hall of Fame Speaker, Author

Explore the five senses with props. Penni Ippensen, LCSW-therapist, introduces sensory activities in her practice and presentations by incorporating simple props. The purpose is to demonstrate how stress can be reduced when our senses are pleasantly activated. Five-pointed, squishy stars help to introduce the concepts. Each point represents one of the five senses: touch, sight, smell, taste, and hear. (See below.)

Play-Doh® by Hasbro or dough uses the five senses through a modeling compound form:

- touch: squishy texture calms as it's kneaded and shaped

- sight: pleasing colors make us happy

- scent: pleasant—at least I think so!

- sound: pat or lightly smacking the substance can be heard.
- taste: non-toxic, but very salty. Not yummy!

Play-Doh® has too many benefits to ignore: fosters creativity, promotes play, eases tension, releases excess energy, improves focus, helps us express emotions, encourages hand dexterity from squishing, rolling, flattening, and shaping. This activity is perfect for geriatric dexterity too.

Blow bubbles: any dollar store will sell bottles of bubbles.

- sight: visually pleasing
- touch: wet solution, may tickle if bubble breaks on your skin
- sound: quiet or you can hear the exhale as you blow through the wand.
- scent: hmmmmm, I may have to get a bottle to sniff!
- taste: soapy

Chocolate kisses:

- taste: sweet or bitter depending on the type of chocolate
- touch: creamy, melted
- sight: smooth or bumpy—if it contains nuts
- sound: quiet or crunchy
- scent: cocoa, roasted, or fruity

Stop & Stomp & Stare:

- Stop what you're doing.
- Stomp your feet to ground yourself.
- Stare to take everything in around you. What do you see and hear?

Ippensen understands the benefits of play for adults. We often stop playing in light of work and family commitments and other obligations. If only we could remind ourselves that the pleasures of play can improve the quality of life at any age! Look at these benefits* of play:

- Relieves stress (You knew that one would be at the top of the list!)
- Improves brain function (cognitive skills, critical thinking, and working memory)
- Boosts creativity
- Enhances social and intellectual growth
- Keeps you feeling young and energetic
- Helps to heal emotional wounds.

*psychologytoday.com

Play is essential for children and adults. It can be an important source of relaxation and stimulation for any age group.

Explore your flexibility at work or play. Do you become frazzled when plans change quickly? Do you need time to process a change in plans or can you go with it?

I believe there are two types of people.

1. those who are comfortable with spontaneity

2. those who need more stability

I'm in the first group. Here are a couple of examples to illustrate that mode.

Tread water through change. My mom was always well-organized and punctual, but sometimes schedules could change quickly. I recall her picking me up from swim practice. Schedule-wise, something had changed. After practice, she poked her head in the locker room and said, "Get dressed! We've got to get going!"

It wasn't that I couldn't hurry, but I'd worn my swimsuit under my clothes to practice, "But Mom, I forgot to bring underpants!"

"Don't worry about it. Models never wear underwear and you'd never know it."

That worked for me. Off we went!

Decades later the tables turned. Mom had taught me well. During winter break, we visited my parents in Naples, Florida. One cloudy day, we were going to the Teddy Bear Museum. While waiting for Granny by her car, the kids and I watched the clouds break apart. The sun came out. We exchanged knowing glances, dashed inside, and jumped into our swimsuits. I grabbed towels and headed back to the car. Soon, Granny came out and noticed we had changed clothes.

"What's happening???" she asked. We'd flip flopped the plans, throwing her for a second.

"Well, the sun came out and now we're going swimming!"

Mom rolled her eyes out loud at me and went back inside to change. She was generally agreeable, because she knows who helped develop my flexibility muscle years before.

Wedding guest takes a pass. One summer day, Jeff and I got home from work and needed to get everybody's clothes changed for a wedding. Korey hadn't worn a dress for a while, so we weren't sure which ones still fit.

"Take off your swimsuit so we can try a couple on to see what works," I said.

She was happy with one dress. We got everyone ready, grabbed a snack, and headed to the wedding for a thirty minute drive. After several minutes into the trip, Korey announced, "I FORGOT TO PUT ON UNDERPANTS!"

I tried to ease her concerns with my own history, using the "Models never wear underwear" theory. (See above story.) Then as little brothers will do, Nick added, "Yeah, Korey, if we see that your dress is stuck in your crack, we'll know why!"

Jeff and I wanted to laugh so hard, but we knew Korey hadn't appreciated his humor..

There's really no point to this story, aside from the fact that, at times, I was a terribly, hurried mother. But we survived, trying to minimize stress along the way. I'm happy to report that, somehow, our children have grown into seemingly stable adults, who, by the way, can change clothes as fast as someone can come up with activities!

Workplace changes. Sudden changes in plans occur regularly in the workplace. This can be unsettling for those who need to sit with the changes and ponder them for a while. Others can quickly adapt to a turn of events. How about you? Are you an adapter or a delayer? When your work environment changes, does it cause you undue stress? Jot down below changes that cause you stress. Sometimes just naming these events can help us be better prepared for them.

_____

_____

_____

Consider the white flag waved! During one weekend, I was on call to service the Bank's ATM. I received frequent, automated calls to fix some sort of malfunction. I became very annoyed with driving back and forth from home to the ATM multiple times that evening and was getting more frazzled by the hour.

I decided to surrender to the problem and chose to stay in my locked car by the ATM while waiting for the next page. I'd read or nap. As I locked the ATM door for the umpteenth time, I glanced across the street at the movie theater marquis. "Top Gun" was showing. I bought a ticket and sat in the back, just in case I got paged again. It must've been agreeable to the ATM muse, because I didn't get one call during the movie! I felt like I'd lost the war, but had won a battle!

"Sometimes when locked into a frustrating situation, we must find a compromise to help reduce the stress."

—Bobbe White, CLL-E, NOCW

It's your turn! Jot a few ideas below that you want to explore. Maybe it's a massage, renting a paddleboat at the park, or waking thirty minutes early one morning to meditate. Go for it!

_____

_____

_____

_____

_____

_____

stress no e**V**il

VENT

When something goes wrong and stress pops in, some of us have a strong urge to act out. It works for me when I'm alone or in the presence of my dog. Mother would be appalled with my language sometimes, but I always feel better afterwards. There are many ways to vent your emotions: shredding, smashing, popping, punching, slinging, and screaming. If you're totally confused, each of these ideas will be explained soon!

The Merriam-Webster dictionary "The letter "V" is never silent." To get the full benefit of venting, you don't have to be silent either!

At this moment, I suspect that you're trying to think of words that start with "V" to see if you can bust this theory. Am I right? It's fine, fun, and good for your mind to try. Typically, however you choose to vent, it will be audible.

JUST SHRED IT!

My friend, Marta, and I were out for a walk when she blurted out, **"SHRED!"**

"What was THAT??" I asked. I stopped in my tracks. I wasn't sure what had just happened. It seemed that she was yelling out loud to herself or somebody.

Marta explained, "When I say, **"SHRED,"** it busts the negative thoughts in my brain. In this case, it interrupts the chain of pain and anger I have for Stuart." Stuart was her ex-boyfriend. I must've looked puzzled. She went on to explain, "This kind of shredding is like paper shredding, except you're disrupting and destroying annoying mind chatter instead of paper!"

I finally understood! She had created a virtual head shred machine!

I shared **"SHRED"** with our bank staff during a wellness session at work. Obviously, it's not professional to use when clients are around, so we practiced it discreetly. A co-worker passed my desk later and said, "There's a lot of shredding going on upstairs!" We both laughed knowingly.

It was both helpful and funny to share this idea. When someone yells, **"SHRED,"** the natural tendency is for everyone to stop in surprise for a nanosecond. They may not know specifics, but they generally understand. It feels supportive. This technique, used to disrupt negative thought patterns, could be considered a cognitive behavioral strategy. (I've had just enough classes and experience in this area to know a little!)

Experts estimate that we have between 50,000-80,000 thoughts a day. Let's stop wasting our precious energy on negative thoughts. Don't feed the beast/message that is looping through your brain. Starve it and replace negativity with something more positive.

You can shout it out or simply think **"SHRED!"** For a more hands on approach, you can write your negative thought(s) on a piece of paper. Tear it into pieces and throw it away or burn it in a fireplace or pit. In Sunday school, we would write something on bread with squirt cheese and then toss it in the river.

JUST SLAM IT!

Another fun way to disrupt a negative thinking loop is with the Dammit Doll. It's a rag doll that I use in my presentations to demonstrate venting with a toy.

An instructional poem is sewn onto its chest. These dolls come in handy for people who are dealing with some type of stress. (Isn't that about all of us? A sample of the doll is shown below.

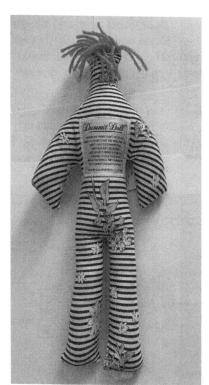

The Dammit Doll poem:

When you want to climb the wall
And stand right up and shout
There's a little Dammit Doll
You cannot do without

Just grasp it firmly by the legs
And find a place to slam it
And as you whack the stuffing out
Yell Dammit, Dammit, Dammit!

Some dolls have an additional stanza:

*"If Dammit isn't a word you say,
then twist its little neck.*

*Grumble out repeatedly,
"Oh Heck! Oh Heck! Oh Heck!"*

JUST SMASH IT is a more physical version of "SHRED." At carnivals, people would pay $1.00- $2.00 to smash old cars with a mallet. Today's version features smash shops that are opening in some cities. Customers pay to enter a special break room to smash plates, glasses, and other breakables. Protective clothing is provided and required. Breakables are aimed at a target (i.e. brick wall.) I love the duality of the break room: a place designated for breaking something and a place to take a much-needed break.

Before throwing, you may write something on the plate, such as someone's name, an illness, or a professional roadblock. Basically, you could write any thought that might be keeping you awake at night. Major issues may require a meat platter; smaller concerns fit on a snack size plate! Groups pay to celebrate birthdays, break-ups, retirements, and other life events. Businesses smash for team building. For some, this concept results in great levels of catharsis and bonding.

Kate Dwyer of Clean Slate (January 7, 2019) interviewed experts about the negative or positive effect of breaking things to ease tension. E. Blake Zakarin, PhD, Assistant Professor of Medical Psychology in Psychiatry at Columbia University Medical Center, suggested, "There's no evidence to support that expressing stress or anger aggressively or physically is super helpful to you." Kevin Bennett, of *Psychology Today* believes smash shops can exacerbate stress and rage in some people. Finally, she spoke with clinical psychologist Scott Bea, who thinks the activity might reinforce negative coping habits.

My unprofessional opinion is this: when people enjoy an activity, like smashing, or whacking the stuffing out of a rag doll, isn't it a form of play? We know that play is an effective stress-relieving approach. Breaking stuff sounded fun to me, so I tested the idea and smashed a partially broken clay pot in a Glad® bag. There was something undeniably satisfying about it.

"With any idea, there will be both positive and negative opinions. Your task is to test the tips and decide which ones work for you."

—Bobbe White, CLL-E, NOCW

If the idea of smashing perfectly good items sounds wasteful to you, consider this: some thrift stores are overflowing in donations and nobody wants Grandma's china anymore anyway. After breaking items, you could always consider repurposing those broken pieces into a beautiful mosaic image or giving new life to a forgotten table in the attic. What perfect symbolism is that? Venting, in whatever form you might choose, is simply one option. Other ways to vent follow.

JUST POP IT! When Amazon delivers a box, grab the bubble wrap! There's a certain satisfaction with popping bubbles. Some call it an obsession! It's hard to explain until you try it. Most people pop the bubbles with their fingers, while others may prefer to stomp or sit on it. My friend, Pattie, gave her mother a roll of bubble wrap for a gift once. What a great gift that is! Grab some bubble wrap, ask your smartphone to play Michael Jackson's song, "Beat It!" When MJ sings, "BEAT IT," just pop it!

JUST PUNCH IT! Are you beginning to sense a pattern here? So far, we've learned that vent can mean multiple things: shredding, yelling, smashing, and popping. Next, grab your pillow and punch it. Scream into it like you mean it! Pound it. Throw it. Grip it. Nobody gets hurt and you may feel better!

JUST SLING IT! During my live presentations, I use a lot of props like this next one, the slingshot stress monkey. Both the slingshot and the Dammit Doll are examples of how we can combine props and play to combat stress.

Slingshot stress monkeys are plush little creatures. To my knowledge, nobody's been injured by one of these flying monkeys yet. They can sling your stress right out of the ballpark—or office. Zing one across the room or against a wall. Special detail: monkeys wear a cape, hat, or mask for smooth sailing.

(Monkeys and Dammit Dolls are both available on the order form at the end of this book.)

"JUST SCREAM IT!" is a hotline that went live in 2020. You can do just that—call and record your scream at (561) 571-8431. Uploaded screams are added to a playlist of more than 130,000. The project, developed by Chris Gollmar, a New York City educator, believed that prior to the November 2020 election people felt like screaming! His assumption was correct: many people felt like screaming about it!

Most calls last only two to three seconds. Gollmar previews them before uploading to the website. A few callers even let a screaming baby contribute. Instead of a scream, you may also leave a message of hope or listen to their daily message of hope. (NPR Jan. 21, 2021)

"JUST TRY IT!"

Dr. Colleen Hacker, Professor and US Olympic Mental Health Skills Coach, suggests that there is one main critical question. "How can we move forward from pain?" Post-traumatic growth. A more recent iteration of post-traumatic growth is stress-related growth (SRG.) SRG is defined as positive outcomes that can result from stressful or traumatic situations, such as:

1. Mastery (getting better at something)

2. Increasing our coping skills (Ability to handle distress) Emma Hays calls it "positive discomfort."

3. Closeness to others: sometimes our most meaningful connections have come from unexpected people, in unexpected places, and in unexpected ways.

4. Spirituality (A new understanding of who I am in this world? What's my purpose? What's my renewed understanding of my life, its value and its purpose?)

The pandemic has given us opportunities to grow. You have to recognize that there is potential growth and it's available to each one of us, regardless of age, gender, or affiliation in life or career, but you have to DO something. It's not something that just happens. Happens is a passive process, You have to actively engage with the opportunity."

"Think of your difficulties like a field of tall grass. Every time you walk on the grass, you create a pathway. The more you walk on it, the flatter and stronger it becomes. Each time we tell our stories of our pain, difficulty, or languishing we strengthen our pathways. You have to look for areas of gain, recognize them, and then make a choice to talk about them and act on the gains rather than continually revisiting the old pathways. This way, you are always creating new pathways of accomplishment."

—Dr. Colleen Hacker, Professor and US Olympic Mental Health Skills Coach, as heard on "Laughter Permitted" podcast May 19, 2021

stress no ev**il**

INHALE

My favorite sound while falling asleep is to hear my dog inhale. It reminds me to do the same. What is more important, especially in times of stress, than deep inhaling—except, maybe exhaling? When we get upset, we become hyper alert. Our body and mind interpret the issue as a true threat, preparing for flight or fight. To conserve energy, our systems prepare for survival mode. One result of this may be shallow breathing.

Flying into a frenzy can make us anxious. Anxiety is a beast that feeds on itself. When not in imminent danger, it's helpful to remember to calm our systems. Start with intentional, methodical, deep, belly breathing. Oxygen will be distributed evenly through the body, and that helps lower blood pressure. As we exit survival mode and regular breathing resumes, heart rate and muscle tension decrease. Deep breathing will help bring calmness to you. Regular practice improves deep breathing.*

The practice of yoga was suggested earlier in the "Explore" section. It has a prominent place in this chapter as well, seeing as the practice incorporates deep, intentional breathing to expand the lungs.

Now, back to that breath. To start, shut your eyes or relax your gaze. Inhale through the nose. Slowly exhale all of your air slowly through your mouth. Envision the tension flowing out during your exhale. For breathing exercises, keep reading.

*Harvard Health Publishing (health.harvard.edu)

To improve deep breathing, have a dress rehearsal instead of a stress rehearsal! That means it's practice time! If you have underlying conditions, consult your healthcare provider first.

4-4-4-4

    a.   Inhale slowly and deeply (through the nose) <u>for four seconds</u>.
    b.   Hold <u>four seconds</u>.
    c.   Exhale (through the mouth) <u>for four seconds</u>.
    d.   Repeat four times.

The Elevator (That's what I call it.)

    a.   Close your mouth.
    b.   Press on the left nostril.
    c.   Breathe in and up through the right nostril. (Going up!)
    d.   Switch and press your right nostril.
    e.   Exhale out, or down, through the left nostril. (Going down!)
    f.   Repeat four times.

E-X-P-A-N-D-A-B-L-E breathing ball

Hold the ball with both hands in front of your face.Pull out/expand the ball as you slowly inhale. Collapse the ball as you exhale. Repeat for several inhales/exhales..

Caution! Expandable breathing balls are highly contagious. Others will become engaged and begin to inhale and exhale with you. It's lightweight, colorful, and effective. Give the gift of breathing. (Pictured below. See order form at the end of this book.)

"EXPANDABLE BREATHING BALL"

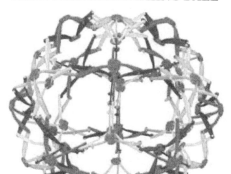

Search online to find additional exercises to practice deep breathing. Below are benefits you can realize from deep breathing exercises:

- Relaxes muscle and mental tension
- Increases oxygen to body systems
- Improves mental concentration
- Lowers blood pressure
- Releases endorphins, the feel-good hormones
- Stimulates the lymphatic system (Detox rocks!)
- Relieves pain
- Full oxygenation improves immunity
- Increases energy
- Improves digestion
- Helps support correct posture

*Andrea Watakins, LCSW

stress no evi**L**

LAUGHTER AND **L**EVITY

First, I want to tell you that I am a Certified Laughter Leader Expert with the World Laughter Tour, Inc. Seriously, I have a diploma and everything. Some call what we do, "laughter therapy." Others just call us crazy. Whatever we're called, we help people regain the practice of laughter when they've become a bit rusty. This practice is done without the aid of comedy or jokes.

Secondly, do I think everything's funny? Of course not. Do I have a fairly good sense of humor? Most people who know me would say, "Yes." What I try to do every day is to stay alert for something humorous.

Levity defined is: "Humor or frivolity, especially the treatment of a serious matter with humor or in a manner lacking due respect." Here's a huge pile of synonyms: lightheartedness, carefreeness, light-mindedness, high spirits, liveliness, cheerfulness, fun, hilarity, mirth, laughter, merriment, comedy, funniness, wit, nonsense, irreverence, flippancy, silliness, and jocularity.

Why is this chapter so lonnnnnnnnnnggggg? As stress tools go, laughter and levity are my personal favorites and I have abundant examples. If it's been a long time since you laughed, remember: it's never too late for laughter!

One cornerstone of my presentation is to spend time around like-minded people (i.e. people with similar interests and a sense of humor.) Someone suggested to me that it would be more accurate to say, "laugh-minded" people. Great idea! I love it when people get my topics better than I do.

This outlook holds particularly true in the workplace. We laughed every day in my office. Some days we even got into trouble for laughing. In our defense, our customers often commented how much they enjoyed coming into an upbeat environment.

With permission secured from my funny friends and family, I've included some of my favorites.

"Humor that makes us laugh is so much more than entertainment! You are literally healthier than you were before laughing, even if you don't know what you are laughing at!"

—Karyn Buxman,
Speaker Hall of Fame, Author, Neurohumorist

Karyn Buxman once spoke to our bank staff about the time that her nursing and teaching career evolved into a speaking and writing career. I thought she'd be a fun person to know, so years later, I asked her to lunch. We reconnected, found several common interests, and two months later, I attended her therapeutic laughter workshop and became one of the first seventy Certified Laughter Leaders in the world! Who knew there was such a thing?

Is knowledge power? Not totally. To underscore her point, Karyn told a story about a patient who had a heart attack. You can know *how* to do CPR, but CPR does the patient no good until you *apply* CPR. While humor is not a life or death matter, the concept for many things is the same, even for laughter. We can understand the benefits of humor, but it's much more effective when we apply it to life. Use it or lose it. If you don't look for the funny, you'll miss the funny. If you don't let yourself laugh, you'll stop laughing.

"You don't have to BE funny as much as you need to SEE funny. "Just be aware! It's everywhere!" To see funny, you just need to listen to what's going on around you and also watch. It takes practice, but it's worth it."

—Karen Buxman,
Speaker Hall of Fame, Author, Neurohumorist

Buxman continued, "The best and safest place to start finding funny stuff is with self-effacing humor. (i.e. humor that makes fun of yourself.) It forces a person to be vulnerable when others witness us doing something wrong, silly, or stupid."

For me, that's an everyday occurrence. My problem was this: I was bad at laughing at myself. I got mad when I felt stupid or embarrassed. Not any more! I've improved, but will always be working on this. Useless stress is part of every activity when you fear doing something imperfect or downright dumb. When you no longer feel guarded, you'll soon have a sense of freedom and a lot less stress in everything you do!

"When it comes to laughing at yourself, do everyone around you a favor. YOU GO FIRST! It sends a message to others that you acknowledge your imperfections. They may be waiting for you to laugh so they can join in support—and relief."

—*Bobbe White, CLL-E, NOCW*

Throughout my stories, you may notice some repeat names. Someone suggested I change a name for more variety, but I decided to leave them as is. This is because some people share funny stories with me more than others. My kids aren't any funnier than your kids. My parents or partner were/are probably a lot like yours. Basically, I began making note of the funny things twenty years ago. And you can too. It's not too late!

Always remember that there is risk in using humor. We think most humor is harmless, but there's always a chance that your humor could be misinterpreted or misunderstood by your audience. Your audience might consist of just one person.

Karyn Buxman shares this next story about a flight passenger in first class. It's a good example about taking the risk in a situation. The flight attendant saw that the passenger's seat belt was unfastened prior to takeoff. She realized the man was Mohamed Ali! Apparently, he didn't think the seat belt rule applied to him, like it did for other passengers.

"Sir, you need to fasten your seatbelt," the flight attendant reminded him.

"Superman don't need no seatbelt." he said.

The flight attendant replied, "Superman don't need no airplane!"

Imagine how many times the flight attendant has had to remind passengers to fasten their seatbelts. Oddly enough, some individuals believe they should be exempt from certain rules. That is typically when tension mounts, stress bubbles up, and tempers can explode!

The flight attendant chose to apply humor to keep the situation from becoming tense. She defused the situation. It worked, but there's no guarantee that it always will. Therein lies the risk.

Be a good sport. Sometimes we leave ourselves open to being the humor target, such as I did in this next story. One evening, when driving down Broadway with Nick, I noticed a businessman walking on the side of the busy street. He carried a gas can and was still in his suit and tie. I recognized him as one of my co-workers.

"Oh look, Nick, there's Glennon, from the bank. Looks like he ran out of gas. Must be heading to his car now."

The next day at work I asked, "Did you run out of gas last night Glennon? Nick and I saw you walking on Broadway."

Glennon asked, "Do you mean you saw me and drove right by me?"

"OH MY GOSH! What was I thinking? I wasn't. In fact, it never *occurred* to me to stop! When we saw you, you were cutting across the parking lot, so I assumed you were close to your car." I tried to justify my logic.

"I was still four blocks from my car!" he said.

Oh boy, did I feel terrible. I'm not sure if I was being selfish with my time as much as I was self-absorbed at that moment. It had been a busy day and with all this traffic, it clearly was a busy evening. But still. BUT STILL. You don't just drive by a friend like I had.

Later that day, I emailed Glennon about something work related.

He replied by signing his email this way, "Brother, Can You Lend A Hand?"

That year at our company holiday party, they gave stupid gifts to people who had done stupid things. I got a gas can and a pair of trifocal glasses so I could see Glennon the next time he needed help.

"When we have to eat crow*, we might as well do so with a smile full of feathers!"

—Bobbe White, CLL-E, NOCW

*Eat crow is an old saying that means, "to admit that one was wrong, or accept that one was defeated, especially when it's humiliating." (merriam-webster dictionary)

One free thing at the hospital is occasional humor. A few years ago, Glennon had a heart attack. Yes, this is the same Glennon from the previous story. He used levity very well to help manage his and his family's stress throughout the ordeal, so he's a good example to prove the theory that humor can diffuse stress.

Cardiologist: "You have arrhythmia. Premature ventricular rhythm."

Glennon: "And I don't even know how to dance!"

Prior to the procedure, Glennon asked the doctor, "Doctor, if I'm not going to make it, will you just whisper in my ear that I had a cute angina?"

Several weeks later, I ran into Glennon at the hospital's E.R. as he sat in the waiting room. The nurse might've thought I was his mother. She invited his son, Myron, and me to follow them to the exam room. She handed Glennon a drab green gown.

"Put this on. Opens in the front," she said.

"Do you have anything in lavender?" Glennon asked.

We all laughed. Stress was instantly defused. Some people use humor naturally to redirect their stress in critical times. It works because when they laugh, we laugh and everybody feels better. Even if it's temporary, it can be enough to put us into a better state of mind.

Not everyone finds levity in tough moments. The point is to be aware of the difference, so as not to be either offensive or offended. We're all different. Something comes over me and my sense of humor pops up in dark times. Please know we aren't trying to dismiss the severity of the situation. It's our means of coping.

More medical humor to wrap around your wounds. The interesting thing about humor is how it can appear when least expected. It's like a gift of fresh air.

Following a stroke, Dad was rushed to the emergency room.

E.R. doctor: "What was happening at home throughout this event?"

Me: "He was falling all over the place. I couldn't get him up off the floor to a chair or to bed. He was like dead weight."

Dad sat nearly straight up on the gurney and said, "Bobbe, I'd really prefer that you use another word besides dead weight!"

Humor moves into the assisted living facility. After a month of hospitalization, Mom and Dad lived at home, with the help of my sister, Cathy. It soon became apparent they needed more help. We moved them into an excellent assisted living home. One afternoon, while folding their towels we had the following conversation.

Dad: "I sure wish I could be of more use to you girls."

Me: "You were, Dad. It's now our turn to be useful to you."

Dad: "But how are you going to be useful if you have another baby?"

Me: "I'm *not* going to have another baby!"

Dad said teasingly: "You don't know… you might change your mind!"

Me: "Dad, I'm 59 1/2 years old. No. More. Babies."

Dad: "I don't know how old you are. Hell, I don't even know how old I am!"

"When it comes to searching for someone with good leadership potential or an online dating match, one of the top three qualities preferred is that the person has a sense of humor."

—Karyn Buxman,
Speaker Hall of Fame, Author, Neurohumorist

This next story is about our previous dog, Lily White. If you're not an animal lover, please bear with me. I know not everyone has, wants, or likes animals. For those of us who do love our animals, it can be nuts how we dote on them. It seems ridiculous how people can melt into sugary syrup over a puppy. I'm one of them. Nothing made us happier at the bank, than when customers brought their pups into our lobby or through our drive-up lanes. They would drool for a dog biscuit. (The dogs drooled, not their humans.) It's turnabout time now and I mentally note the drive-up businesses who give my puppy treats. It makes me happy. Pets also make us laugh. I hope your pets make you laugh too.

Lily was no exception. We have more funny memories than there are kibbles in the bag. Lily was a rascal, always stealing Jeff's possessions because he left them within her reach. She'd then dash outside with her prize to taunt him. Her top three preferences were:

- TV remote
- Cell phone
- Jeff's glasses

His glasses (AKA readers) were my personal favorites because Lily looked very smart when she held them in her teeth, as seen in the photo below.

"Now let me think. How should I reconfigure these?"

A typical conversation would unfold like this:

Jeff: "Dammit, Lily, drop it!!"

Me: "Don't leave your stuff where she can get it!"

Jeff: "She should know!"

Me: "She's a *DOG*!"

Fortunately, Jeff buys cheap glasses, because Lily confiscated a lot of them. Thanks to Lily, most pairs now sit comically crooked on Jeff's face. He leaves them on even when he's not reading. Imagine how difficult it is for me to keep a straight face during a serious conversation—which most of Jeff's are!

Next to pets, kids are right up there to make us laugh. First Art Linkletter showed us the funny side of kids on his show, "Kids Say the Darndest Things!" Another show, "Little Big Shots" is a riot too. Check it out if you want to see some funny stuff.

Counting is fun in any language. And funny too:
"Uno, Dos, Tres, Crotcho, Stinko."

—Brooklyn, age 5

Let's try harder to forget about our busy-ness and take time to listen to the kids. There's so much humor to be enjoyed. If we don't write their quips and quotes down, they'll be lost forever. Share your stories. Who knows? It may help the next person recall one of their own stories, too.

Elsa, you're the best—but just for a bit. Disney's *Frozen* was the theme for Madelyn's fifth birthday party. A teen dressed up as Queen Elsa. She helped as hostess, server, gift handler and even pusher on the swings outside.

After a bit, Madelyn said, "Elsa, you can leave now. I kinda just want to play with my friends."

THAT's what I call, "Getting right to the point!"

If nothing else, kids are honest! Our son, Nick, toured the Mormon Temple, in Nauvoo, Illinois, with some friends.

On the return trip, his friend, Skip, asked, "What religion are you?"

Nick answered, "Well, my mom's Jewish and my dad fishes." (And hunts and...) #truth.

84

They say it how they see it. Korey, once asked me, "Where's that school form you signed?"

"It's in my office," I said.

"Mom, we're trying to figure out which room in this house ISN'T your office!" #ouch

Junior jocks suit up. When Nick started YMCA football, parents were asked to purchase accessories, such as jock straps. Off we went to the sporting goods store. We found the protection section, only to find the variety to be overwhelming.

A sales clerk approached us and asked, "Ma'am, can I help you find something?"

"Yes, I'm looking for a jock strap for my son," I said as I pointed to Nick. He was a small boy at age nine.

The clerk eyeballed Nick and agreed, "Okay, so you need a jockstrap and a cup, correct?"

"Yes, a jockstrap...but a cup???" I asked. I was confused.

"Ma'am the cup is the protective part. The jockstrap holds it in place," the clerk explained.

"Ohhhhhh! Got it." I said. I felt like a total idiot.

Next, the clerk asked, "What size do you think he'll need?"

I shrugged, "I have no idea. Do you maybe have something in a training jock?" I mean, they have training bras for girls don't they?

The clerk stifled a smile, "Based on his apparent size, let's start with an extra small."

We paid for our purchase, took the bag and headed home. I dropped the package on the kitchen table where Jeff was sitting and said, "Next time, Buddy, you take him!"

Jeff opened the package and inspected the purchases. He held them up, "Honestly, I don't even know why they need to wear these things. They don't even dangle yet!" (Below: me while jock-strap shopping.)

"I SAID I'M DOING THE BEST I CAN!"

Volunteering can be funny too. My friend, Nancy, helped at a dance for adults with special needs. She wanted everyone to feel included, so she canvassed the room to encourage more people danced.approached Ronnie. She felt kind of sorry for him, because he sat all alone on one of the chairs that were lined up around the room.

"Ronnie, would you like to dance with me?" she asked encouragingly.

Ronnie answered earnestly, "I was hoping for somebody a little younger."

#nowwhoisthewallflower

Travel humor

It was a warm, spring Easter Sunday in the midwest; the kind of day that motivates people to hit the gardening departments, myself included.

Meanwhile, Korey and her friends were in Las Vegas for spring break. She sent a text and a screenshot of her beautiful brunch at the Bellagio Hotel & Casino. That was some fancy food!

I was in a long checkout line at Home Depot. Since the line was five customers deep I had time to text her back.

"Your brunch looks fantastic! I, on the other hand, am waiting in line at Home Depot to buy a hoe. I guess that makes me an Easter hoe-er."

Her answer sent me into hysterics: "You should see all of the Easter whor-ers out here!"

Naturally, everyone stared at me because of my outburst, but you just can't worry about a bit of random laughter, you know?

Winter causes fog warnings. When Jeff and I travel by car in the winter months, I get the same response every time that we get in. While getting settled, the windshield always fogs up.

Jeff always tells me: "Bobbe, turn on the defroster. You're breathing too much!"

Oh, gosh, so sorry. I'll stop.

Don't forget to pack your humor. Traveling or living abroad has additional hurdles, such as language barriers, that makes life more interesting.

Tanner moved to Japan to teach English as a second language. He face-timed his mom one morning with a Kleenex® stuck to his chin. His mom realized he had a small cut and suggested a Band-Aid® because Kleenex® looked dumb.

"I ran out of them. I'll run to the 7-Eleven store and buy more and some New Skin® Liquid Bandage too."

Later, Mom checked on Tanner. The tissue was still stuck to his chin.

"No Band-Aids®?"

"I tried," he said, "but my Japanese isn't good and I ended up with wood glue and condoms!"

"WHAT? Show me the packages," Mom said.

Tanner held them up to the camera.

"That's crazy! The condom box DOES resemble a box of Band-Aids®. Good luck with those on your face! As for the wood glue, maybe you'll have some furniture to repair."

Recap: if you're going to travel internationally, first pack your sense of humor. You'll need it.

My go-to gifts for high school graduates were either tool kits or study lamps. Having a graduate gift shelf minimized shopping time, which I found as a plus. Our kids thought this was boring because there was never any surprise—for them—when our gift was opened.

We attended a graduation party for our friend, Meredith. I wrapped a desk lamp and we headed to the party. When it was time to open gifts, we gathered around her.

"Thank you. I love it! It's perfect for my dorm room next year," said Meredith.

Nick punctuated the conversation by saying, "That's what my mom gives everybody."

It's true. I do.

The "Magnificent 7" women's Olympic gymnastics team captivated the country in 1996. Our Korey, like thousands of smitten little girls, was glued to the TV. If you followed the games, you may remember a few of the popular crew: Danielle Moceanu, Shannon Miller, and Kerri Strugg.

Gymnasts begin and end their routines by presenting briefly in the "salute" position. To salute, you stick your chest out, arch your back, extend your arms with hands in the air, palms facing outward. Legs and feet are straight and held tightly together—without wobbling—for at least two seconds.

Korey stood in front of the TV in her tiny leotard and asked, "Mom, why do gymnasts always smile their tush when they present?"

"Smile their tush?" I asked. "What does that mean?"

She explained, "It's when they stand there and present, it looks like their tush is smiling."

"Show me," I said to Korey.

She pushed her chest out, arched her back, and threw her arms up in a "V". Then she turned around with her backside to me.

"See Mommy, when you stand still and present, it looks like their tush is smiling."

Ahhhhhh! I could see it. By golly, when she tightened her muscles, her tush WAS smiling! It was a little curve from cheek to cheek. Only a seven year old would see a smile in all of that effort. The next time I was in front of a mirror, I turned around to see if I could "smile my own tush." (I'll bet you will try it too, or you already did, right?) But alas, it was somewhat of a half-smile, on its way to a grimace. No Olympics for my tush!

Here's your sign. Another simple way to find some humor is by keeping an eye out for funny signs. This includes billboards, bumper stickers, and license plates. (Sometimes I make my own fun by pulling over and taking the suggestion literally.)

"Hostess on duty, please wait to be seated." This was the typical sign inside the main doors of The Eagles Nest, a fabulous little bistro in Louisiana, Missouri. The flip side of this was in the restroom. The first thing you noticed was a framed sign perched on the top of the toilet tank:

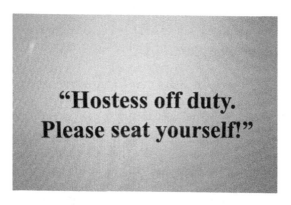

(Hostess off duty sign is available on the order form at the end of the book.)

Dark Humor *(AKA Gallows Humor)*

Humor can occur during dark times—if you're open to it. You can also count on being tickled by dark humor at the least appropriate time. If and when this happens, it's important to remember and understand that not everyone shares the same sense of humor.

Do you ever wonder if your higher power has a sense of humor too?

I vote, "YES!" There was some unexpected levity during Dad's burial in February 2018. It started when it was time to lower his casket into the grave. At some services, the casket is not lowered until everyone leaves the cemetery. Jewish law believes that leaving with the task unfinished is considered to be an affront to the deceased.

At this point, let me introduce our friend and funeral director, Jeff Spear. So we don't confuse him with my husband, Jeff, I'll refer to Jeff Spear as J. Spear.

The casket was lowered on long straps that resembled a seat belt. They are connected to a tension-controlling device. When the casket reached the bottom of the grave, J. Spear slid his strap out and rolled it up easily. The vault attendant struggled. Wilbert, (not his real name) couldn't tug, jiggle, or wiggle his strap out from under the casket. It was stuck. Why didn't he just cut it or throw it in the hole? But Wilbert never gave up. An awkwardness filled the air.

Unexpectedly, Wilbert jumped into the grave, right on top of Dad's casket! We heard his boots land on the hard surface. Jeff and I glanced at each other wide-eyed and tried turning our attention back to the front. We watched him climb out of the hole, like it was a swimming pool. He had freed the strap and carried it out with him. It was a bizarre scenario!

The funeral service continued until a small, plastic cap from the lowering device fell into the hole next. Wilbert groaned loudly, "Arrrrrrgggghhh." He jumped back into the grave!

Jeff and I locked eyes again. This time, it was more in amusement than amazement. I checked on our grown children behind us. Being their first Jewish burial, they were unsure about the norm. Logic told them this wasn't it.

Staying composed was terribly difficult. I held the program under my eyes. Tears flowed freely. I do not have to tell you that these were *not* tears of grief. Our daughter and daughter-in-law, Korey and Jenna, stifled giggles behind us. We were a collective mess. The book title, *Hop on Pop*, by Dr. Seuss, kept popping into my head. My warped sense of humor was in full throttle. This is both a blessing and a curse. We struggled between snickers and sniffles until service concluded.

Afterwards, I approached Jeff S. "I'm sorry our family appeared less than reverent, but that was pretty funny." On that chilly February day, J. Spear replied, "I did get a little warm myself." As the director, I'd have sweated too.

We knew that we'd witnessed something unusual. When friends asked me, "How'd it go?" I couldn't help but retell Wilbert's snafus and we'd end up laughing together.

Years later, I still mentally replay this event. Aside from the honor guards, twenty-one gun salute, and the playing of Taps, little else about Dad's service makes me feel sad. For that, I am thankful. For some of us, at least, humor and laughter are truly therapeutic.

But it was more than that. I believe Dad's spirit was present throughout the burial. He always had the best sense of humor! On numerous occasions, he and I would laugh ourselves to tears at things nobody else found funny.

Friends who heard the story agreed that if the tables were turned and Dad had attended a funeral like this, he, too, would've been laughing and crying.

Some of the relatives in attendance missed the snafus completely. Other relatives who had witnessed the activity, failed to find it as funny as my immediate family had. The processing of these events underscores a primary premise of humor that not everyone will share a similar sense of humor. This is particularly noticeable with dark humor.

"Often, contrasts bring art to life: the bright speck of paint on a dark canvas; the tightrope walk between humor and tragedy."

—Laura van den Berg

Everyone decides for themselves whether something is funny or not. Obviously, something as common as grief will have varied responses. I was thankful and relieved that Jeff and our kids had processed the incident as I had.

Were these signs from above? People speak of signs that are sent from the deceased: a rainbow, bird, butterfly, or even a clap of thunder. I believe Dad definitely sent us a sign that day. I look at it as more of a gift than a sign. This last gift of his to us was the gift of humor and to remind us that it is possible to feel the lightness of humor, even while feeling the heaviness of grief.

Kids of the Office Humor

One Friday, I had a half day off, so I went swimming. Afterwards, I went to the grocery store. I threw on a sundress over my swimsuit. After swimming, my hair was flat. My make-up was long gone. Then again, it was summer. I thought those things were expected and acceptable.

In one aisle, I met my co-worker, Dot, and her five-year-old daughter, Kaylee. We chatted about how work had gone for her that afternoon. She asked about my half-day off. I felt Kaylee looking at me with curiosity. With a five-year-old's honesty, Kaylee asked Dot, "Mommy, is she laid off?"

Apparently, my casual look was teetering on the edge of scruffy. I'll have to work on that.

More Sports Humor

In fifth grade, Nick weighed about seventy pounds. And THAT was with all the football equipment on! One game, they played a team with very big players. In fact, one player was a 223 pound fifth grader! (We should've asked for his driver's license to see his actual age.)

Our team lost terribly: 40 - 0. Afterwards the coach huddled the team together before releasing them to their families. They dragged their feet on the long walk to us. My dad asked Nick the question: "Did anybody get hurt really bad today?"

Nick answered, "Yeah, one kid got bronchitis."

Class humor: they heard it at home

It was parents' visitation night at Korey and Nick's school. Korey was in third grade and doing well with her daily journaling. Maybe a little too well, because here's one entry we read: "When I grow up I want to be a gymnast so I can go to the olympics. No, I think I'd rather be a man. Because it's a man's world." #wonderwheresheheardthat

As I was saying, they heard it at home...

When Ben was three or four, he had an imaginary career at JCPenney.

When asked if his store was in the mall, he told his grandma, "No it's in the jungle."

"Really, it's in the jungle? Why do you say that?" Grandma asked.

Ben: "Cause it's a jungle out there when you have to go to work every day!"

Ice cream is the right answer to everything! As a little boy, Ben participated in pee-wee soccer. One night he didn't particularly want to go. His dad reminded him:

Dad, "Ben, what are we going to do if we win today?"

Ben, "Get ice cream!"

Dad, "What are we going to do if we lose today?"

Ben, "Get ice cream!"

Dad, "Okay then let's go play soccer!

That, right there, is about two scoops of positive attitude!

You say, "Nothing's funny?" I beg to differ. Can't find *anything* to smile or laugh about? Certain Youtube videos always work for me. Some of my favorites follow:

- Brides can't stop laughing. (The 9/5/2009 clip is my personal favorite.)
- Funny puppies/babies
- The Weatherman can't stop laughing.
- Steve Harvey interviews kids.
- Grandma reads *Wonky Donkey.*
- Teacher's COVID-19 song makes news hosts craugh (cry and laugh.)
- Funeral mourners can't stop laughing.

Some of these clips may seem rude or even irreverent to you. They are funny to others, because of the times when it may have been an inappropriate time to laugh, but it couldn't be controlled. Plus, laughter is very contagious, which, of course, doesn't help.

She was enthused when she wanted to be. Mom turned 96 on September 3, 2020. Due to the pandemic, the best Cathy and I could do was to visit her in the nursing home gazebo in the courtyard. Mother had a hearing deficit, so she couldn't hear us from six feet away, nor could she read our lips due to our masks. To help us converse, I brought a white board and markers.

We kept questions short, such as, "How are you?" and "Have you had lunch?" I always asked about her favorite activity, "Did you get your nap?" She typically answered with a nod, shrug or an eyeroll. Finally, I wrote on the board: "Happy 96th birthday!"

Mom's eyes popped wide open in disbelief.

We smiled and nodded.

She rolled her eyes out loud at us and said, "I got old!"

To put it in perspective, I wrote, "Cathy's almost 70!" and Bobbe is 65!" She opened her eyes widely in disbelief at these statements too! Other than that, we had gotten little response from her. When our twenty minute time limit ended, we said goodbye, blew her kisses, and headed for our cars. Fifty feet or so away, Cathy's husband, Dennis, stood by the car. He had waited for us since only two people could visit at a time.

Dennis yelled and waved from the parking lot, "HI GRANNY! HAPPY BIRTHDAY!" He had worn a magenta colored shirt, so he was easy to spot.

We looked at Mom to see if she had seen him. To everyone's surprise, she was waving back at him as if she was queen of the Rose Bowl parade! You could tell by her eyes that she was smiling under her mask. Cathy and I were disappointed that we hadn't been able to elicit a more enthusiastic response. We felt that we'd failed her birthday visit, but decided that it was a good thing someone had been able to spark her day.

A month later, Mom lost interest in food, drink, and staying awake. When she stopped loving chocolate, we knew it was getting close to the end. She died peacefully on October 29, 2020 in the middle of the night.

We donated Mom's clothing to the nursing home before I realized we should've kept her black slacks for her forever outfit. I had multiple reasons as to why I didn't want to go shopping for new pants:

- Avoid shopping during the pandemic
- Avoid running into acquaintances at a time like this
- Unfamiliar big box store floor plans, making the process more difficult.
- T.J. Maxx, thrift or charity stores are tricky, when shopping for something specific.
- Amazon had delivery constrictions with our timeline
- Walmart: nope. Sorry, I'm afraid Mom was a princess. We couldn't bear to bury her in Walmart clothing for eternity. I know that sounds snooty, but, as the saying goes, "You have to know your customers!"

Later on, I stood in the center of my laundry room. A pair of black slacks that were hanging on the clothing rod caught my eye.

"Hmmmmmmmmm," I thought. "Could those work? Those *COULD* work!" There was one concern. Were black leather pants on a 96 year-old inappropriate? Did it really matter? I weighed my argument: the pants were the right color, the brand was agreeable, I avoided shopping (yay!), and the stupid leather pants had never fit me well anyway (boo!)

My friend, Carol, made me buy them at a St. Louis upscale, resale shop. The problem with the pants is the waist snap popped open if I sneezed, coughed, or laughed. Still, I hung on to them for some reason. This must have been it!

Was black leather too racy for Mom? On the plus side, she had lost a lot of weight and they definitely wouldn't pop open. I delivered the pants to the funeral home. Marcus took them from me and raised his eyebrows a bit, but he didn't judge—out loud anyway.

I smile whenever I think about those pants. Mom was *always* very well-dressed. This outfit was no exception! I was relieved to get buy-in from the family. We all agreed that Dad would love seeing Mom again with her young lady look in her snazzy leather britches. Giddy-up Mom!

The 'A' team

Because of my story above about the bumbles at Dad's burial, you can imagine the tension we felt when Mom's casket was being lowered into the grave. Would the vault employee jump in again? I feared our family might lose control. We held a collective breath and finally shared a sigh of relief when things went smoothly.

There was one thing, though. This vault employee was a tall, lanky, agile, gentleman. He straddled the grave, with one foot on either side of the opening. It was so wide, it reminded me of him having one foot on the Missouri side of the Mississippi River and the other foot on the Illinois side. It was THE widest stride I'd ever seen on a man. He was practically doing the front splits! I may have uttered an audible, "WHOA!" To say the least, it was an impressive position.

After the funeral, I mentioned to J. Spear., "This went better than Dad's."

"Yes it did! We brought our 'A' team today!" he said. "That other guy didn't last long." I can't imagine how Wilbert's references would read: "Jumps immediately into problems as needed."

Expectant humor

No, this part isn't about pregnant women, although there are many stories on the topic. What I meant by expectant humor is this: tomorrow Snow White and I are going for a walk with one of my best buds, Tammy, and her dog, Ernie Banks. (Tammy's dad played, scouted, and coached for the Chicago Cubs. Hence, Ernie Banks is her dog's name.) I go for the guaranteed laughs, because we always do. Sometimes we rant, but mostly, we'll laugh at the absurdity of most things. Here is my favorite Tammy tale.

We were into the fifth of a six hour drive to Indianapolis.

Me: "Oh no! I might have left my phone in the restaurant in Danville!"

Tam: "Should we go back?"

Me: "No, that's too far, it's too late, and I'm too tired to turn around."

Tam: "Okay, I'll call you and if we hear your ringtone, we'll look for it at the hotel."

She called me and we heard my phone ring until it finally went to voicemail. Oh, thank heavens for small favors. We finally arrived at the hotel, opened the car doors for light, and swiped under and between the seats and around the floor mats.

"YES! Here it is!" I announced with great relief. "Oh no...I missed a call!"

Tammy glanced at my phone and then looked at hers, "You ding-a-ling, that was ME!!!"

We started laughing, which turned into crying or craughing. (Laughing + crying = craughing!)

We were a hot mess of laughter, fatigue, and tears as we approached the check-in counter. The hotel receptionist asked, "Long trip, Ladies?"

You know what they say, "The last twenty yards are the longest!"

It was the first time I got investment advice from my OB/GYN. After a biopsy, I received my physician's report. It started out fairly normal, but I was laughing out loud by the end. Years later, I found the letter and shortly thereafter, I ran into the now retired, Dr. Lou DeGreeff, and we laughed about his letter. He gave me permission to reprint it here.

> *"Dear Bobbe,*
>
> *I have received the results of your recent biopsy. Everything looks fine without evidence of any problems. My only recommendation is to buy low and sell high!*
>
> *Sincerely,*
>
> *Louis E. DeGreeff, M.D."*

I recently shared this story with a friend. Oddly enough, she had her own letter from Dr. Lou. And that's exactly how humor continues to entertain us. If each one shares one, our stories live on and they will remind us of something funny that we might have forgotten along the way. Here's the next letter:

"Dear June,

I have received the results of your mammogram. The radiologist and I both agree, your breasts are quite remarkable."

Sincerely,

Louis E. DeGreeff, M.D.

Hopefully, you weren't offended by either of these letters. The point of sharing them is this: many medical tests and exams can be nerve wracking, before, during and after the procedure is finished. If some humor falls your way that could ease your anxiety, why wouldn't you want to be open to it? Clearly, my tendency is to welcome the humor, rather than refuse it.

"When you let others know you're open to (most) humor, life becomes more fun. It's not joke-telling really, but simply observing life's daily opportunities. Own your own bloopers. Be observant every day.

—Bobbe White, CLL-E, NOCW

So much humor, so little time

Believe me when I tell you I have volumes of journals filled with humor nuggets. Many of them won't be shared; they're just for me. There have also been lapses in my life when I neglected to note the humor. Sadly, those may never be recovered. I hope that you start—or continue—to mine the humor that you encounter every day.

How can I add to my humor arsenal? I'm going to restart my journal engine and enter something daily. Will you join me? I keep a little one in the car as well. I used to keep one in my desk drawer at work. You never know when or where the next nugget of humor comes from!

Daily Rx.

Debbie is my cousin-kind-of-person. Our families have been friends for over a half century or more. I know Debbie will always answer her phone in the wee hours of the morning, because she's on eastern time. I love hearing her giggle. And it doesn't take much! It always keeps me on a good track to connect with her/them.

Michele is another early morning positive buddy! And she's not even on eastern time. Michele is the voice of laughter and logic. We can laugh at just about anything. One of my biggest pleasures was to introduce Debbie to Michele at Nick's wedding. They both have healthcare backgrounds and a dark sense of humor, like me. Both are far wiser, kinder, and more giving than I could ever be! Keep your positive connections close.

Find daily distractions. Dr. Colleen Hacker, US Mental Health Skills Coach, emphasizes the importance of finding daily distractions. Humor is just one form of a daily distraction. Your kids, dog, cat, bird, or goldfish can be other forms. We all need that one thing that can briefly take us away from our real tasks and worries. This is where I believe my tips have application. As difficult as they are to wedge into already full schedules, daily distractions can be very effective in our efforts to manage stress. It just takes a moment of your time. You're worth a moment, aren't you?

(Not) Fun Facts

- The National Institute of Health (NIH) estimates 75% of all doctor visits have a tie to stress. Did you know it was that high? In terms of diagnoses with a link to stress, heart disease is number one, followed by high blood pressure, stroke, obesity, respiratory disease, insomnia, depression, skeletal problems, digestive issues, complexion problems, cancer, and reproductive problems.

- NIH also stated that 50% of industrial accidents are caused by the stress of personal problems, which people carry to work.

"If you don't make time for your wellness, you will be forced to make time for your illness. Read that again!"

—Unknown

STRESSALOGUE

stress-uh-log

noun (my book, my word)

Defined: a section at the end of the book designed to wrap up the loose ends and answer any remaining questions the reader may have. It's called "Stressalogue" for another reason. Hopefully the tips you read will help end your haggling with stress each time it arises. Think of the tips given here as resources. Test them. Adopt them if they work; dump them if they don't serve you well. Our lives will never be free of stress, but you already knew that. Heck, if I could do that for you with this book, I'd be queen of the world and we already have Beyoncé for that.

Is it stress-worthy? Make this your top-of-mind question when you feel stress coming on. The issue bothering you isn't stress-worthy to me. It's how *you* interpret and process the issue(s).

To get another take on how to handle your stress in order to live a calmer, saner life, consider the following suggestions.

Sage Robbins, wife of renowned life coach, Tony Robbins, learned to monitor and break her patterns of dramatically over-reacting to improve her inner peace. She gave voice to the times when she heard herself overreact, "You're being dramatic again!" Saying this calms her down.

"We can't change the things that people do or say, such as when you're behind a slow driver when you're in a hurry. There are over 700 billion things happening around us. What matters is what's going on inside of us."

—Michael Singer, Author of The Untethered Soul

Why is managing stress a perpetual challenge for so many of us?

I've tried to say, in various ways, that we are all wired differently. What works for me may not work for you. In fact, what works for me won't *always* work for me! Let me repeat that.

"What works for me may not work for you. What works for me won't always work for me. Over time, situations change. We change. Our resources must also."

—Bobbe White, CLL-E, NOCW

In my endless exploration for stress-conquering attempts, I've tried spinning, sitting, singing, acting, running, walking, talking, whining, wining, drumming, painting, crafting, napping, coloring, puzzling, cooking, cleaning, driving, swimming, Zumba-ing, Pound® class, yoga, pilates, and tamales! I'll keep adding to my arsenal. I hope you will too!

Last month I landed on a new stress-tool activity: book folding. Perhaps it served as a diversion tactic to keep me from working on this book. It's tough to know how and when to end a book. Not only did this activity provide me with a diversion, but also a shower gift I needed to give. Then I decided it could also be a segue to end this book!

Let the heart pattern remind you that unmanaged stress is hard on your heart!

The other reason for including the heart book here is to express—in something other than traditional words—**how grateful I am to you for reading it!**

My parting words (I promise!) are these: when writing a book, the topic is often on my mind. I start finding tie-ins to songs I hear and things I see. Everything seems to relate to the book's theme. Kenny Rogers' refrain came to mind when folding the pages of the heart book. I also realized the song had application for what we should do with our stress.

"You got to know when to hold 'em and know when to fold them. Know when to walk away, know when to run....Now every gambler knows that the secret to survivin' is knowin' what to throw away and knowing what to keep."

—Kenny Rogers, "The Gambler"

I sincerely hope that you will find it easier to walk away from stressful situations and determine which events or individuals are toxic, before succumbing to them. Embrace it or dump it!

Here's wishing you less stress and more joy,

Bobbe

A little more…

about the cover

This section explains the idea behind the use of monkeys, in general, and the creation of Stress No Evil, in particular.

Why monkeys? I like finding images for intangible concepts, such as stress. I thought about the metaphor, 'monkey on your back.' It originally referred to having an addiction and later became more applicable to carrying a burden that cannot be easily gotten rid of or solved (i.e. problems or situations that make us unhappy for a long time.*) That seemed to fit the problems associated with stress.

The 'monkey on your back' idea then went to a swimming pool. Imagine swimming with children. They are playing around you, when one child scurries onto your back and up to your shoulders, just like a monkey. Little bodies are slippery when wet, yet kids somehow manage to hang on forever. You cannot shake this monkey off your back! While sitting atop your shoulders, the child may need to hold onto something. This can result in a tight grip on your neck or forehead. Yay.

Your shoulders begin to tire as you cough, sputter, and gurgle from the neck grip. If the grip is on your forehead, it can feel like a gymnast's ponytail that's been pulled too tight and for too long. Relief only comes when the child jumps or falls off of you.

Compare the idea of the child on your back to a problem weighing on your mind. Sooner or later you will need or want to unload the burden.

From the pool to the three wise monkeys. In the next section, you can read more about the history of the Three Wise Monkeys. You learned earlier why I added the fourth one!

This information is for those who are not familiar with the Three Wise Monkeys. Otherwise feel free to move on.

The Three Wise Monkeys are known individually as Hear No Evil, Speak No Evil, and See No Evil. If this is a generational concept with which you're unfamiliar, below are various meanings ascribed to the monkeys, both interpretative and cultural.

A. Hear No Evil

Don't listen to gossip or believe everything you hear. Don't hear what you want or hope to hear. Truly listen, don't just hear. Confirm what you hear. Don't assume. Don't eavesdrop. Listen to what you hear but keep an open mind. Listen between the lines. Listen to the thoughts we put into our minds ourselves, also known as "Mind Chatter."

B. Speak No Evil

Don't speak badly of people. Or to people. Don't promise what you can't deliver. Don't gossip. Think before you talk. Don't lie. Okay, go ahead and lie, but say "Hello!" to Karma. Who's Karma? She's a world class witch, that one is. Her mantra is, "What goes around, comes around." Remember: Karma never forgets an address. Don't speak over people. Or down to them either. Try not to speak before thinking. Don't interrupt.

C. See No Evil

Don't stare or glare at people. No one likes to get the stink eye. That's rude at any age. When you observe something, don't assume you immediately understand the situation. When conversing with someone, don't look down on or past her or him. Don't judge people by his or her appearance.

What's the purpose of the Three Wise Monkeys? The idea is to encourage us to tap into our moral compasses to become more aware of what we say, see, and hear. When it doesn't feel right, it usually isn't. You may have an unsettled feeling about what you just experienced. It can work on you constantly. My stomach feels like there's a brick sitting in it. When I wake up, my focus moves right to the issue that's been bothering me. This is what stress feels like to me.

Recently, I posted this question on Facebook:

"In six words or fewer, what do you do to manage your stress?"

Here are the answers, in alphabetical order of first name, last initial.

A
Alana F: I say my prayers!
Amy B: Read, exercise, wine, put stress in perspective
Amanda D: car wash!
Anita M: pray, see family/friends, and look up!
Addie S: give thanks and forgiveness
Ann M: take a walk listening to music
Alex G: long drive on a winding road
Anonymous: profanity, alcohol, eating and slug like habits
Anne V: simplify, get quiet, focus inward, sleep
Amanda V: treat myself to drive-thru coffee
Andrea C: positive self-talk, journaling, walk, tea, sleep

B
Barb H: meditation, good food, practice gratitude, and, oh...chocolate!
Bobbe W: car wash, play with my pup, walk, swim
Becky M: walk in my garden, dig in the dirt
Billy S: basketball & smoking
Belinda C: gave up drinking alcohol

C

Char S: Think good things, breathe, appreciate the basics
Chris E: dance
Connie M: deep breathing
Charlie M: walk in faith first
Carol B: Chin up, just keep moving
Chris W: daily devotional, exercise
Carol W: carbs, whine to friends, work
Connie H: chocolate, dog snuggles
Carol R: wine, meditate, more wine!
Connie W: give it to God
Colleen C: breathe, pray, cry, laugh, socialize
Carri B: Lots of prayer

D

Debra F: I say the serenity prayer
Debbie M: prayers, family, essential oils
Debbie M: snuggle and play with grandbabies
Danni M: deep breathing, golden retriever snuggles
Doreen H: lay quietly, close eyes, breathe, pray
Denise S: breathe, affirm problem,move forward, know all is in divine order
Deanna H: walking, listen to music
Diane E: identify the real emotion
Donna S: grandkids remind me of my purpose
Donna T: think good thoughts that happened, breathe
Dave F: exercise and whiskey!
David O: exercise daily, breathe, focus, laugh often!
Doris M: movement
Dan B: drugs, sex, and rock 'n roll
Diane J: wine x 6
Donna B: color therapy, create, sew beautiful fabric

E

Erin C: replace negativity with a grateful heart
Ellen C: family, yoga, pets, pray, walk, gratitude
Ed G: exercise vigorously, problem solve, order varies.

F:

Frankie G: breathe in, breathe out, just breathe.

G

Gary M: breathe, list gratitude, help others
Gwen B: I walk 2-3 miles daily
Gretchen E: watch feel good movies
Gina V: pray and talk to Brian

H:
Halie H: music and animals
Harry M: think of good positive memories

I-J:
Jenna W: exercise and dog snuggles
Jenna H: music
John B: breathe, remember I'm retired
Jean M: daily outdoor walks
Jean M: Tai Chi
JoAnn W: "Do not worry about anything." Philippians 4:6
Janet P: deep breathing, prayer, walk in nature, dog snuggles
Jane G: I practice mindfulness, breathing activity
Jacci A: breathe!
Jan H: Zumba, and reading every night
Jenny H: Enjoy God's beautiful creations with prayer
Judy B: take a hot bubble bath
Julie A: Quiet time with good thoughts, relaxing
Jane H: pickleball, yoga
Jacqueline J: pause, breathe deep, think good thoughts
Jayne S: say prayers, drink wine, friends
Jane G: breathe and read
Jan H: Zumba
Janet P: deep breathing, drinking water, prayer, nature
Julie H: clean!

K
Korey W: yoga, reading, therapy
Krista L: exercise, dog snuggles, music
Kathy W: yoga, wine, dog, activity, pray
Kathy R: crochet, ride my bike
Kara: writing about it, yoga, dancing
Kathie M: wine, beer, crying, music
Karen J: daily walks, talks, eating gardening
Kathryn F: I breathe and go to God!
Kristin W: Prayers and kindness to others
Kathy W: create and play with elements of art
Kevin H: "Will it matter in five hours, weeks, or months?)

L
Lyndsay L: exercise, reading, and puppy snuggles
Laura T: walk outside listening to nature
Linda C: always fresh flowers during quarantine
Laurie B: shopping, traveling, Pilates
LeAnn Z: I like to laugh too!
Liz S: think best/worst outcomes, make a plan

Lenny B: live in a state where weed is legal
Lon C: Serenity prayer, pray, breathe
Lisa W: hug my husband, pet dogs.
Lisa S: think about tomorrow and the goodness in my life
LeeAnn H: breathe deeply, music, wine, family, friends
Lori C: stretches and daily workouts
Lisa P: deep breathing, connecting,writing,

M:
Marilyn K: yoga, meditation, cook, wine, whine
Mark C: I simply remember my favorite things...
Michael K: Take a walk and smile
Mary D: call high school friends or co-workers
Marianne P: outdoors, music, dance, write, exercise, vent
Michelle B: laugh, gratitude, nature
Monica H: prayer, exercise, quiet, good nutrition, rest
Mary Beth M: yoga, long walks, praying, friends, nature
Mary B: gratitude, perspective, prioritize, clarity, energy
Mike M: take a nap
Martha D: Jammie day!
Mary M: get lost in a good book
Martha R: living into love
Myra K: faith and quiet prayer
Mary S: take a walk, God's beauty soothes
Marty D: prayer
Mary A: music and plans for a better day
Mary I: I cry a lot.
Mary V: Think of my grandkids

N:
Nancy B: talking with husband, play with dog, pray
Norma H: deep breathing, a Manhattan a day!
Nora B: peel foil, twist wire, pop cork!
Nancy T: hug my big white horse
Nancy G: with prayers

O-P
Pattie P: prayer, exercise,
Pat M: walk, read, meditate, pray, think of family
Peggy K: pray, be grateful, exercise, family time
Pam A: nature
Patty M: walk outside or exercise
Penny L: just breathe, look for the bright side
Penny K: get outside
Peggy P: exercise, music, sister chats, outside
Penni: breathe, pray, create, wine, family, create again

Q-R
Rochelle B: music
Rob T: Listen to Foo Fighters
Rod W: Find a good listener, a dog is best.
Renee S: vodka shots and sun
Randy P: Stress can be a focus tool
Rajah M: breathe, sleep, stretch, eat, take magnesium

S
Sheila D: have a snack, take a nap
Susan L: cuddle with my black Lab
Shelly S: meditate, exercise, pray
Sarah K: let go and let God. Amen!
Sue D: play with grandchildren
Spencer D: play with the dog
Sarah K: prayer meditation, service to other
Sandy B: Cuss!

T
Tim B: work out, go outside, spend time with Marilyn
Terry A: go play with Quest horses
Tammy M: craft & sew!
Theresa Q: stay active, keep connecting, respecting, reflecting
Tracy H: walk my dogs, morning church time
Tootie M: laugh
Tarri C: bake, nosh on it, my hub paints, plays pianos
Tracy S: breathe, walk, talk, read, write, pray. (Repeat.)

U-Z
Vickie W: Friends, family, doggy, exercise, pray, wine,
Vicki E: exercise, thankful journal
Vicky A: smile and deep breathing
Val S: deep breathing, prayer, pet Scarlet, walk

In six words or less, how do you manage your stress? If this is your book, list them below. If not, you can list them elsewhere. (How about in your phone notes?) Remember: use them as needed. If they're not serving your well, find some new ways!

1._____   2._____

3._____   4._____

5._____   6._____

Bobbe White is an empowerment expert, author, speaker, and Certified Laughter Leader. (Seriously!) She has been speaking professionally for over twenty years to employees of organizations and association members who want to better manage their stress and find more joy in the workplace, the home place, or basically any place. Bobbe accomplishes these objectives through sharing real life experiences and laughter therapy.

Bobbe believes the application of humor can help us put most situations into perspective, thus making them more manageable. Bobbe was interviewed about "Laughter in the Workplace," by the New York Times, Newsweek Japan, Rediff-India, and Family Circle. She has traveled the country in all directions to dispense her fun and functional presentation.

She and her husband, Jeff, live in Quincy, Illinois with their newest therapeutic tool named, Snow White, the black Lab. (It was either that or Betty White.) Bobbe recently retired from banking after a forty year career. She worked through four decades, four economic swings, and four hair colors. Bobbe and Jeff's family includes Korey and her fiancé, Spencer and Nick and his wife, Jenna. They each have their own therapeutic tools as well. When we all gather at this White house, it's a three dog night.

"Guy"
(Korey & Spencer)

"Molly"
(Nick &Jenna)

"Snow"
(Bobbe & Jeff)

One. More. Thing.
Haiku by Busy Bobbe

Just one more thing before I leave.
So important
so it seems.

The stoplight ahead teases yellow.
Just get through.
Ugh. Turned RED.

White knuckles grip the wheel
Blood pressure rises
like a hot air balloon.

Wait, wait, wait, wait, wait
Wait, wait, wait, wait, wait, wait wait.
Wait, wait, wait, wait, wait.

Begging out loud for the light to change.
Drivers stare.
I glare.

I'm mad at stoplights.
At clocks
and myself.

The red light turns green.
Our turn.
MoveMoveMove!

They move so slowly.
Wasn't anyone ready?
Blood pressure rises.

Nobody else cares.
Because they aren't
late.

Thoughts turn to why I'm late.
Everyone knows the truth.
It's Busy Bobbe.

I bargain with myself.
I promise to stop doing
One. More. Thing.

CONTACT BOBBE:

Mobile: 217.242.3705
Email: bobbewhite@gmail.com
FB: bobbewhite
IG: bobbewhite
Twitter: @bobbewhite
LinkedIn: bobbe white
Blog: bobbewhite.wordpress.com

Laura Gramke is from Quincy, Illinois. She graduated from Western Illinois University, with a B.A. Studio Art and moved to Orlando to be a Walt Disney World cast member. She performed in multiple parades. Laura then became an American Airlines domestic and international flight attendant. Then the pandemic slowed air travel. Laura and tens of thousands of flight attendants were furloughed indefinitely.

Davidson, North Carolina, is home base, along with her fiance, Pat. Laura returned to her artistic tendencies, painting watercolor portraits of pets, homes, and abstract objects. Her company is named ElleGee Design. Laura soon connected with Ashley Martin, another furloughed flight attendant. The two created custom paper goods (i.e. stationery, all-occasion cards, and painted decor.) In their new business, "Standby Paper Goods," Laura is the artist; Ashley is the wordsmith. They are "on call for your greeting card needs."

Laura and Ashley have turned their passion for connecting with people worldwide into a stationery endeavor, "Hanging up our panty hose and accepting home base has brought us to the realization that planes are not the only way to connect with the people who matter!"

After painting the White family dogs, Bobbe asked Laura to create illustrations for this book. I hope you have enjoyed her work on these pages.

CONTACT LAURA:

Web: ellegeedesign.com
IG: @ellegee_design
Pinterest: @lauraelizabethsusan
Etsy: ElleGeeDesign
IG: @standbypapergoods
Etsy: StandbyPaperGoods
Web: standbypapergoods.com

Bill Beard is a transplant from Pittsfield, Illinois, to Quincy. He graduated from John Wood Community College with an A.A.S. in graphic design. Bill has worked in a variety of graphic design positions, from photoengraving and paste-up to digital work on his much beloved Apple computers. He also freelances as an illustrator, and can be found at various local festivals and special events drawing caricatures for the public. A cartoonist since he was seven, Bill has produced a weekly editorial cartoon for his hometown newspaper since 1987, and has self-published cartoon collections of his semi-daily comic strip, *The Adventures of Marty and Turkey.*

CONTACT BILL:

Mobile: 217.257.6719
Web: billbeard.graphics
Email: wjbeard@icloud.com
IG: @bbeardcartoonist
FB: martyandturkey
LinkedIn: bill beard

Life in the Laugh Lane
Steering through life's twists and turns with laughter!

~

If Stress is Garbage, I've "BIN" There, Recycled That
Tips for going green to reduce your stress,
recycle your laughter, and repurpose your life when life overflows!

~

Alphabetiquette(Booklet)
Couth after youth

Contributing author:
Chicken Soup for the Wine Lover's Soul
Fantastic Customer Service, Inside and Out
The Ultimate Gardener
Priceless Personalities

This page is dedicated to those individuals who create in any form and who have trouble knowing when a project is perfect "enough" to be done. You know who you are. This monkey's for us!

ORDER FORM

PRODUCT DESCRIPTION	QTY	TOTAL COST
STRESS NO EVIL PAPERBACK @ $11.95 EA		$
STRESS NO EVIL COLORING BOOK @ $5 EA		$
STRESS NO EVIL BUNCH OF QUICK-REF TIP CARDS @ $10		$
SLINGSHOT MONKEY @ $10 EA		$
EXPANDABLE BREATHING BALL @ $10 EA		$
HOSTESS OFF DUTY FRAMES 4" x 6" @ 3 for $10		$
LIFE IN THE LAUGH LANE $10 EA		$
IF STRESS IS GARBAGE, I'VE 'BIN' THERE, RECYCLED THAT @ $10		$
CHICKEN SOUP FOR THE WINE LOVER'S SOUL @ $15		$
ALPHABETIQUETTE: (booklet) Couth after youth @ $5		$
THE BUNCH! Stress No Evil book, coloring book, quick-ref deck of cards, breathing ball, slingshot monkey @ $45		$

Snail or Email this completed order form to Bobbe, or send a screenshot of your completed order form to: 217.242.3705, or

> **Make order form with check payable to:**
> **BOBBE WHITE**
> **1313 SO. 29TH ST.**
> **QUINCY IL 62301**
>
> **Venmo: Bobbe White**
>
> **Debit or credit:** CCN: _____
> EXP____/_____   SIC: _____   ZIP CODE: _____

☐ **Shipping address is the same as billing.**   ☐ **It's a gift! Ship it to the following:**

Name _____

Address _____

City _____ **State** _____ **Zip** _____

Need a card enclosed? You've got it! Write your message below:

_____

CLOSING WITH COLOR

A coloring book fills the remaining pages—and this page too! Feel free to color or decorate the letters as well. The back of each page is blank for your own creativity. Or... On the back of each page is a question or two about the tip. Extra space is on the back to write (about anything), doodle, or draw. While coloring, tune in: how you are feeling? Is coloring fun? Do you feel calm(er?) Also, go wild with color! Monkeys, bananas, and letters can be *any* color or pattern: striped, plaid, or polka dotted! Use crayons, colored pencils, markers, or watercolor. Perfection is not required.

There aren't any rules! Hello, happy! See you later, stress!

WHO DOESN'T LOVE TO COLOR?

STRESS

NO EVIL

NAMASTE

What are your favorite sounds?

_____

_____

_____

_____

What sounds do you find annoying?

_____

_____

_____

_____

SOUND!

Where do you find quiet?

_____

_____

_____

_____

Is there a place that's quiet that you haven't been, but might try the next time you seek silence?

_____

_____

_____

_____

SILENCE!

Are there people or places that you would call "Toxic?" Explore which ones are toxic to you and why it seems that way. If you feel safe writing them here, do so. Otherwise, just give the topic some thought so that you're better aware.

Toxic Person's Name	Reason
Example: Aunt Clarice	Too bossy. Makes me feel dumb.

Toxic Place's Name	Reason
Example: Cave	Dark, echoes, bats overhead

AVOID TOXICITY!

**How do you—or can you—rest best to get back your zest?
(Sorry, I can't resist a rhyme!)**

_____

_____

_____

_____

_____

REST!

RELAX!

If going solo is awkward for you, try it once. Note below what you did alone. Would you try it again? Is there something else you might do solo?

_____

_____

_____

_____

_____

ROLL SOLO!

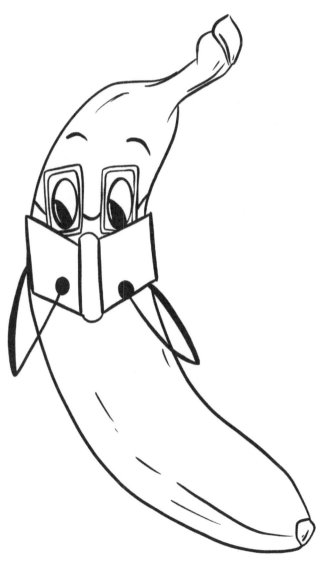

If you're more of a loner, who could you call?
Where can you find people?

_____

_____

_____

_____

_____

GET SOCIAL!

What or where do you—or could you—scrub?

_____

_____

_____

_____

_____

How can you incorporate more bubbles in your world?

_____

_____

_____

_____

_____

SCRUB!

Have you tried saying, "NO" with some of the suggestions given?

_____

_____

_____

_____

_____

Do you know of some other ways to say, "No?"

_____

_____

_____

_____

_____

What do you like to do outside?

_____

_____

_____

_____

_____

What else can you try to do outside?

_____

_____

_____

_____

_____

GO
OUTDOORS!

What is at least one activity that you would consider trying?

_____

_____

_____

_____

_____

EXPLORE!

How do you—or could you—vent in a healthy way?

_____

_____

_____

_____

_____

After breathing deeply four or five times, write down how it feels:

_____

_____

_____

_____

_____

INHALE!

What's one funny thing that happened today? (It only matters that it was funny to YOU!)

_____

_____

_____

_____

_____

Name at least one person who always makes you laugh:

_____

_____

_____

_____

_____

LAUGH!

THE

END!